Debating Globalization

Debating Globalization

DAVID HELD *et al.*

polity

First published in 2005 by Polity Press

Polity Press
65 Bridge Street
Cambridge CB2 1UR, UK.

Polity Press
350 Main Street
Malden, MA 02148, USA

ISBN: 0-7456-3524-5
ISBN: 0-7456-3525-3 (pb)

A catalogue record for this book is available from the British Library and has been applied for from the Library of Congress.

Typeset in 10.5 on 12 pt Plantin
by Servis Filmsetting Ltd, Manchester
Printed and bound in Great Britain by MPG Books Ltd, Bodmin, Cornwall

For further information on Polity, visit our website: www.polity.co.uk

www.openDemocracy.net

Contents

Notes on Contributors

Kofi Annan, born in Ghana, is the seventh Secretary-General of the United Nations. His first term began on 1 January 1997, and he was appointed for a second term in 2001, to run until 31 December 2006.

Benjamin Barber is the Gershon and Carol Kekst Professor of Civil Society at the University of Maryland and a principal of the Democracy Collaborative, with offices in New York, Washington and the University of Maryland. His books include *Strong Democracy* (1984) and *Jihad vs. McWorld* (originally published in 1995, with post-9/11 edition in 2001).

Anthony Barnett is the editor of openDemocracy and a non-executive member of the council of Charter 88. He is the author of *Iron Britannia* (1982) and *This Time* (1997); editor of *Power and the Throne* (1994) and co-editor of *Town and Country* (1998).

Patrick Bond is a political economist and global justice activist. He directs the Centre on Civil Society at the University of KwaZulu–Natal in Durban, South Africa. Among his books are *Unsustainable South Africa* (with Simba Manyanya) (2002), *Zimbabwe's Plunge* (2003),

Against Global Apartheid (2003) and *Talk Left, Walk Right* (2004).

Maria Livanos Cattaui has been Secretary-General of the International Chamber of Commerce (ICC) since 1996. As chief executive of the world business organization, she is responsible for overseeing global policy formulation and representing the interests of world business to governments and international organizations. Prior to joining the ICC, she was Managing Director of the World Economic Forum.

Meghnad Desai is Emeritus Professor of Economics and was formerly director of the Centre for the Study of Global Governance at the London School of Economics. He is a Labour Party peer in Britain's upper house of parliament. His latest book is *Marx's Revenge* (2004).

John Elkington is a co-founder and chair of SustainAbility, and a world authority on business strategies in the areas of corporate responsibility and sustainable development. His books include the *Green Consumer Guide* (1988) and *Cannibals with Forks: The Triple Bottom Line of Twenty-First Century Business* (1997).

Thomas N. Hale is a graduate of the Woodrow Wilson School of Public and International Affairs, Princeton University, where he continues as Special Assistant to the Dean. His research interests include globalization and global governance.

David Held is Graham Wallas Professor of Political Science at the London School of Economics. His books include *Democracy and the Global Order* (1995), *Models of Democracy* (1996), *Global Transformations* (with others) (1999) and *Global Covenant* (2004).

Caspar Henderson is openDemocracy's Globalization Editor. He is an award-winning writer and journalist on environmental affairs. Caspar has also worked as a consultant to various government and international organizations, voluntary groups and others on issues in energy, water, regulation, technology, human rights, economics and the environment.

Takashi Inoguchi is Professor of Political Science at the Institute of Oriental Culture, University of Tokyo and former Assistant Secretary-General of the United Nations. His many publications include (co-edited with Purnendra Jain) *Japanese Foreign Policy Today* (2000), (as editor) *Japan's Asian Policy* (2002) and (co-edited with Saori Katada and Hanns Maull) *Global Governance: Germany and Japan in the International System* (2004). He appears occasionally as a commentator on BBC, CNN, and CNBC Asia.

Mary Kaldor is co-director of the Centre for the Study of Global Governance at the London School of Economics, and Professor in the Department of Government and Development. Her books include *New and Old Wars* (1999) and *Global Civil Society* (2003).

David Mepham is an associate director of the Institute for Public Policy Research. He is the co-author (with Jane Cooper) of a recent IPPR report, *Human Rights and Global Responsibility: An International Agenda for the UK.*

Roger Scruton is a philosopher, farmer and businessman. He is Professor of Philosophy at Buckingham University and co-founder of the Conservative Philosophy Group. He runs an international consultancy company, and is the author of twenty-nine books, including *On Hunting*

(1998), *The Meaning of Conservatism* (3rd edn, 2000), and *The West and the Rest: Globalization and the Terrorist Threat* (2002). He is an external editor of the Ecology and Place theme at openDemocracy.

Narcís Serra is president of the CIDOB Foundation, based in Barcelona. He was Deputy Prime Minister and Defence Minister of Spain. He has also served as Mayor of Barcelona.

Anne-Marie Slaughter is dean of the Woodrow Wilson School of Public and International Affairs at Princeton University. She recently served as president of the American Society of International Law and is on the board of the Council on Foreign Relations. She has written or co-edited four books and many articles for scholarly and legal journals, and she is a regular contributor to many newspapers, including the *New York Times*. She recently published *A New World Order* (2004).

Grahame Thompson is Professor of Political Economy at the Open University. He is the co-author (with Paul Hirst) of *Globalization in Question: The International Economy and the Possibilities of Governance* (1999) and *Between Hierarchies and Markets: The Logic and Limits of Network Forms of Organization* (2003).

Martin Wolf is associate editor and chief economics commentator at the *Financial Times*. His latest book is *Why Globalization Works* (2004).

Preface

The principal challenges of our new century are global in scope. They demand the cooperation of people around the world in sustained, serious engagement across differences of belief, identity, nationality and authority.

This is the contention of openDemocracy. We are not alone in believing this. On the contrary we are using the web to pioneer partnerships that can assist the development of intelligent, open politics which measures up to the challenges of our time.

It was in this spirit that, during the summer of 2004, we were delighted to cooperate with Polity Press, and commission a debate around David Held's ideas in his book *Global Covenant*. We linked this to our work with the UN Foundation, as it sought public understanding of the issues behind Kofi Annan's appointment of a High-Level Panel on Threats, Challenges and Change to report on the future of the United Nations in an age of new terrorist threats.

David Held wrote an essay to start the discussion, developing and elaborating his argument. His critics differ sharply on the challenges globalization presents – including on trade, the role of international institutions and the capitalist system. They also contest the solution he advocates, posing issues of national democracy, regional collaboration and global accountability. But all share a

commitment to constructive engagement. Their debate –
by turns stinging, lively, unexpected, rigorous – forms the
core of this book.

openDemocracy has found that the most clarifying
arguments are seldom between those who are furthest
apart. There is often more to learn from exchanges
between those who share enough to respect, and therefore
really engage with, each other's differences.

This is the case with this volume, *Debating Globalization*.
It takes the exchanges published on openDemocracy a
stage further with new contributions by Benjamin Barber,
Takashi Inoguchi, Anne-Marie Slaughter and Thomas
Hale, and Narcís Serra, and a new response by David Held
himself.

The work at openDemocracy continues. One example is
a debate on the future of politics and citizens seen through
the eye of political parties in an age of globalization. This
and other material is available at www.openDemocracy.net.
Please visit the site, join the debate and support our work.

Anthony Barnett and Caspar Henderson

Acknowledgements

openDemocracy is a web-based forum that seeks to promote open politics and the creation of a thoughtful and connected global community. Its principal aim is to use the web to build and map intelligent discussions.

openDemocracy would like to thank David Hayes especially, for his consistent editorial support; Margaret Spillane and Nicola Wissbrock; and David Held and the team at Polity – as well as, above all, the contributors to this volume.

David Held wishes to thank Ellen McKinlay, Neil de Cort, Ann Bone and Breffni O'Connor for all their help and professional support at Polity Press.

1

Globalization: The Dangers and the Answers

David Held

Washington-led neoliberalism and unilateralism have failed the world. It is urgent that we find a way beyond their legacy. This calls for a new model of globalization that works for humans everywhere. In this opening chapter, David Held provides a unified critique of the present global order and sketches his alternative.[1]

1 The crisis of globalization

Over two hundred years ago, Immanuel Kant wrote that we are 'unavoidably side by side'. Since Kant, our mutual interconnectedness and vulnerability have grown in ways he could not have imagined. We no longer inhabit, if we ever did, a world of discrete circumscribed communities. Instead, we live in a world of what I like to call 'overlapping communities of fate' where the trajectories of all countries are deeply enmeshed with each other. In our world, it is not only the violent exception that links people together across borders; the very nature of everyday living – of work and money and beliefs, as well as of trade, communications and finance, not to speak of the earth's environment – connects us all in multiple ways with increasing intensity.

The word for this story is 'globalization'. It is not a singular, linear narrative, nor is it just a matter of economics. It is cultural as well as commercial and in addition it is legal: it is about power as much as prosperity or the lack of it. From the United Nations to the European Union, from changes to the laws of war to the entrenchment of human rights, from the emergence of international environmental regimes to the foundation of the International Criminal Court, new political narratives are being told – narratives which seek to reframe human activity and entrench it in law, rights and responsibilities that are worldwide in their reach and universal in their principles.

The development of this process and the international institutions that embody it began in the immediate aftermath of formidable threats to humankind – above all, Nazism, fascism and the Holocaust.

After 1945 there was a concerted international effort to affirm the importance of universal principles, human rights and the rule of law in the face of strong temptations simply to ratify an overt system of great power interests favouring only some countries and nations. The traditional view of national and moral particularists, that belonging to a given community determines the moral worth of individuals and the nature of their freedom, was rejected. Instead, the principles of equal respect, equal concern and the priority of the vital needs of all human beings were affirmed. The irreducible moral status of each and every person was placed at the centre of significant post-Second World War legal and political developments.

Half a century on, the international community has reached its next clear moment of decisive choice. I am an optimist. I am confident that it is still possible to build on the achievements of the post–Second World War era. The proposals that I advocate, and the direction that I argue the international community should take, are easily within our grasp economically and technically. Politically, they demand new efforts, skill and above all a shared will to achieve them. They are not utopian or unrealistic in the sense of being impractical or beyond our mental and physical resources – on the contrary.

But it is especially important for those of us who are optimists of possibility to be clear about the dangers and difficulties. A combination of developments points towards a catastrophic combination of negative factors which could lead us into another century marked by war, massive loss of life and reckless and destructive violence. We are at a turning point. It will not be measured by days or months, but over the coming few years between now and 2010 choices will be made that will determine the fate of the globe for decades to come. It is that serious.

Just note, by way of introduction, four major ongoing developments I will return to in a moment, each reinforcing the other, all pointing in a negative direction:

- the failure to move towards the United Nations's Millennium Development Goals which set the minimum humanitarian levels for large sections of the world population;
- the potential collapse of the regulation of world trade, and the clear danger that trade negotiations could worsen not redress global inequality;
- the complete failure to address the awesome consequences of global warming;
- the erosion of the multilateral order symbolized by the United Nations but extending through a whole series of international agreements and agencies.

The signs are not good, therefore. The postwar multilateral order is threatened by the intersection and combination of these crises that are taking place simultaneously at the humanitarian, economic, environmental and political levels. The crisis in each is likely to exacerbate the others. More serious still, there is a driving force taking them from bad to worse. This force is willed, even though it often presents itself in the form of inevitability, and it can be summed up in two phrases: the Washington economic consensus and the Washington security agenda.

I will take a hard look at them both. Any assessment of them must be grounded on the issues each seeks to address. But they are also now connected, if distinct, drivers of the specific form of globalization which the world is being forced to experience. Together they have become a combined assault on the principles and practice that began to be established after 1945. Together they promulgate the view that a positive role for government is to be fundamentally distrusted and that the sustained application of internationally adjudicated policy and regulation threatens freedom, limits growth, impedes development and restrains the good. Of course, neither exhaustively explains the current structures of globalization, but they form the core part of its political drive.

It does not follow that, in terms of economics, what the Washington Consensus opposes is good, any more than it follows that the critique of the present working of the UN and international system associated with Washington's security agenda is entirely false. On the contrary, a merely conservative resistance to them that seeks to hold on to the status quo would also fail to deliver what the world badly needs.

Both need to be replaced, and in their place the world needs a progressive framework that:

- encourages and sustains the enormous enhancement of productivity and wealth that the global market and contemporary technology make possible;
- ensures that the benefits are fairly shared and addresses extremes of poverty and wealth;
- provides international security which engages with the causes as well as the crimes of terrorism, war and failed states.

I will call the approach that sets itself this task social democratic globalization and a human security agenda.

Four crises, one challenge

But before outlining what this framework needs to deliver, and why the current one fails, I give a reminder of the four major current crises in the condition of humanity, trade, the environment and current global governance, which make the call for the creation of a better kind of globalization imperative.

First, very little progress has been made towards achieving the Millennium Development Goals. These set down minimum standards to be achieved in relation to poverty reduction, health, educational provision, the combating of HIV/Aids, malaria and other diseases, and environmental sustainability. They are the moral consciousness of the international community. Progress towards the millennium targets has been lamentably slow, and at current rates they will be missed by a very wide margin. In fact, there is evidence that there may have been no point in setting these targets at all, so far are we from attaining them in many parts of the world.

Second, the collapse of the trade talks at Cancún raised the possibility of a major challenge to the world trading system. At the same time, a large growth in bilateral trade arrangements and preferential trading agreements singled out some nation-states for particularly favoured treatment by others. If growth in such bilateral agreements were to continue, there would be a real danger that the Doha trade round would collapse – or produce derisory results.

Recent trade negotiations have made progress on the phasing out of vast subsidies offered by the Organization for Economic Cooperation and Development (OECD) countries to their agricultural and related sectors, but there is no clear timetable attached to the implementation of many of the key points. There are many risks involved, the most serious being to the world's poorest countries. They cannot alone overcome the handicaps of a world trading system marked by rigged rules and double standards. If the world's poorest countries (along with many middle-income nations) are to find secure access to the global economic order, they require a free and fair footing to do so. The slow progress on trade talks signals that they may not reach this point.

Third, little, if any, progress has been made in creating a sustainable framework for the management of global warming. The British chief scientist, David King, warned in January 2004 that 'climate change is the most serious problem we are facing today, more serious than the threat of terrorism'. Irrespective of whether one finds this characterization accurate, it is the case that global warming has the capacity to wreak havoc on the world's diverse species, biosystems, and socioeconomic fabric. Violent storms will become more frequent, water access a battleground and the mass movement of desperate people more common.

The overwhelming body of scientific opinion now maintains that global warming constitutes a serious threat not in the long term, but here and now. The failure of the international community to generate a sound framework for managing global warming is one of the most serious indications of the problems facing the multilateral order.

Fourth, the multilateral order is being gravely weakened by the conflict in Iraq and the American administration's response to the terror attacks of 9/11. The value of the UN system has been called into question, the legitimacy of the Security Council has been challenged and the working practices of multilateral institutions have been eroded. The arrogance of the great powers has dramatically weakened international law and legitimacy, and the prospects for combating global terrorism have been lessened not improved.

How do we address problems on this scale? The economic, political, social and environmental fortunes of all countries are increasingly enmeshed, but the richest and the most powerful nations are not dedicated to building an international order which delivers relief, hope and opportunity to the least well-off and those most at risk, even though this is in their own interests, as well as being in line with their expressed values. A global commitment to justice is essential to ameliorate the radical asymmetries of life chances that pervade the world.

We need structures as well as policies to address the harm inflicted on people and nations against their will and without their consent. Instead, while there is a high degree of interconnectedness in the world, social integration is shallow and a commitment to social justice pitifully thin. Why? I will focus here on two reasons above all others: the old Washington Consensus, and the new Washington security agenda. These two hugely powerful policy programmes are shaping our age and profoundly weakening our public institutions, nationally and globally. Only by understanding their failures and limitations can we move beyond them to recover a democratic, responsive politics at all levels of public life.

David Held

2 The Washington Consensus

The Washington Consensus can be defined as an economic agenda which advocates the following measures:

- free trade;
- capital market liberalization;
- flexible exchange rates;
- market-determined interest rates;
- the deregulation of markets;
- the transfer of assets from the public to the private sector;
- the tight focus of public expenditure on well-directed social targets;
- balanced budgets;
- tax reform;
- secure property rights;
- the protection of intellectual property rights.

A combination of most or all of these measures has been the economic orthodoxy for a significant period of the last twenty years in leading OECD countries, and in the international financial institutions. It has been prescribed, until recently without qualification, by the International Monetary Fund (IMF) and World Bank as the policy basis for developing countries.

The 'Washington Consensus' was first set out authoritatively by John Williamson.[2] While Williamson endorsed most of the approaches listed above, he did not advocate free capital mobility.[3] His original formulation drew together an agenda which he thought most people in the late 1980s and early 1990s in the policy-making circles of Washington DC – the Treasury, the World Bank and the IMF – would agree were appropriate for developing countries.

Subsequently, the term acquired a sharply right-wing connotation as it became linked to the policies of Ronald Reagan and Margaret Thatcher. They emphasized free capital movements, monetarism and a minimal state that accepts no responsibility for correcting income inequalities or managing serious externalities.

There were important overlaps between the original Williamson programme and versions of it which came to be called the neoliberal agenda, including macroeconomic discipline, lauding the free market economy, privatization and free trade. Today, however, Williamson distances himself from the neoliberal definition of the Washington Consensus, although he accepts that it was this version, with its endorsement of capital account liberalization, which became the dominant orthodoxy in the 1990s. I will use the term Washington Consensus in the latter sense: to refer not to the theory, but to the policies of American administrations and their close allies and associated institutions.

Critics charge that the measures of the Washington Consensus are bound up with US geopolitics, and are all too often preached by the US to the rest of the world but not practised by it, and worse, are deeply destructive of the social cohesion of the poorest countries. Interestingly, Williamson holds that while aspects of such criticism of the neoliberal version are true, his policy recommendations are sensible principles of economic practice that leave open the question of the progressivity of the tax system.

Indeed, some of the proposals and advice of the Washington Consensus may be reasonable in their own terms. Others are not. Taken together, however, they represent too narrow a set of policies to help create sustained growth and equitable development. Crucially, the Washington Consensus underplays the role of government, the need for a strong public sector and the requirement for multilateral governance. Put into effect its policies can have disastrous consequences for the capacity of public institutions to solve critical problems, national and global.

The Washington Consensus and development

The relationships between the Washington Consensus, economic liberalization and development have been extensively examined. The focus has been on how the Washington Consensus has been implemented through loans and debt rescheduling that require developing countries to undergo 'structural adjustment' – the alignment of their economies to the requirements of the core policies – and on the subsequent results. Some very serious issues have arisen. They have been summarized pithily by Branko Milanovic in the form of three questions: [4]

- Explain why, after sustained involvement and many structural adjustment loans and just as many IMF standbys, African GDP per capita has not budged from its level of twenty years ago. Indeed, in twenty-four African countries, GDP per capita is less than in 1975, and in twelve countries even below its 1960s level.
- Explain the recurrence of Latin crises, in countries such as Argentina, especially when just months prior to the outbreak of such crises countries were being praised as model reformers.
- Explain why good 'pupils' among the post-Soviet Union transition countries, such as Moldova, Georgia, Kyrgyzstan and Armenia, after setting out in 1991 with no debt at all, and following all the prescriptions of the international financial institutions, find themselves ten years later with their GDPs halved and in need of debt forgiveness.

Something is clearly awry. The dominant economic orthodoxy has not succeeded. Instead, it has failed to generate
sustained economic growth, poverty reduction and fair
outcomes. The diagnosis of the Washington Consensus is
misleading and its prescriptions are damaging.

In particular it has been found that one of the key
global factors limiting the capacity of the poorest countries to develop is the liberalization of capital. Geoffrey
Garrett has shown that what hurts developing countries
is not free trade but the free movement of capital.[5] The
neoliberal Washington Consensus recommends both.
While tariff liberalization can be broadly beneficial for
low income countries, rapid capital liberalization can be
a recipe, in the absence of prudential regulation and
sound domestic capital markets, 'for volatility, unpre-
dictability and booms and busts in capital flows'. Countries that have rapidly opened their capital accounts have
performed significantly less well in terms of economic
growth and income inequality than countries that have
maintained tight control on capital movements but cut
tariffs.

Joseph Stiglitz affirms that both the crises in East Asia in
the late 1990s and the recent recessions in Latin America
show that 'premature capital market liberalization can
result in economic volatility, increasing poverty, and the
destruction of the middle classes'.[6] And a study by IMF
economists published in March 2003 itself finds that 'there
is no strong, robust and uniform support for the theoretical argument that financial globalization per se delivers a
higher rate of economic growth'.[7]

Even more troubling, the IMF study concludes that
'countries in the early stages of financial integration have
been exposed to significant risks in terms of higher volatility of both output and consumption'. Yet, knowing this, the
Bush administration is still leading the way in demanding

David Held

tough capital liberalization through international financial institutions and bilateral trade agreements.

As a result the governing capacities of developing countries can be seriously eroded. This is not to say that developing countries do not need access to capital flows, whether public or private. They do, especially during trade liberalization when imports initially tend to rise faster than exports. But private market capital flows are often both too low and too volatile to provide for such financial needs.

The experience of China and India – following the earlier trajectories of Japan, South Korea and Taiwan – shows that countries do not have to adopt, first and foremost, liberal trade and/or capital policies in order to benefit from enhanced trade, to grow faster and to develop their industrial infrastructure so as to be able to produce an increasing proportion of national consumption. All these countries, as Robert Wade has recently noted, have experienced relatively fast growth behind protective barriers – growth which fuelled rapid trade expansion, focused on capital and intermediate goods.[8] As each of these countries has become richer, it has then tended to liberalize its trade policy.

Accordingly, it is a misunderstanding to say that trade liberalization as such has fuelled economic growth in China and India. Rather, these countries developed relatively quickly behind protective barriers, before they liberalized their trade. Clearly, if these countries, and others like them, did not develop as a result of straightforward trade liberalization, and if it is also the case that some of the poorest countries of the world are worse off as a result of an excessively fast integration into the global capital market, then there is an overwhelming case for applying the precautionary principle to global economic integration and resisting the developmental agenda of the Washington Consensus.

Internal and external economic integration

While economic protectionism should be rejected as a general strategy because of its risks of creating a vicious circle of trade disputes and economic conflicts, the balance of evidence is clear. For a country to benefit from sustained development, its priority should be internal economic integration – the development of its human capital, of its economic infrastructure and of robust national market institutions, and the replacement of imports with national production where feasible.

Initially, this needs to be stimulated by state-led economic and industrial policy. Greater internal economic integration then helps generate the conditions in which a country can benefit from higher external integration, as Robert Wade has shown.[9] The development of state regulatory capacity, a sound public domain and the ability to focus investment on job-creating sectors in competitive and productive areas – all this is far more important than the single-minded pursuit of integration into world markets.

The alternative to the Washington Consensus is not a simple endorsement of state-centric development, nor is state intervention always progressive and beneficial just because it runs counter to it. Rather, the Washington Consensus has eroded the ability to formulate and implement sound public policy and has damaged essential political capacity. Public objectives, for example, can be delivered by a diversity of actors, public and private, with partnerships between them – and not just by the state. The wider development of civil society (trade unions, citizen groups, non-governmental organizations (NGOs) and independent institutions) is indispensable to a robust programme of national development. Of course, there will be conflicts between economic development and the strengthening of civil society. But societies need significant measures of autonomy to work out their own ways of managing these conflicts.

There is, in fact, no single preordained route to or set of policy prescriptions for economic development. Knowledge of local conditions, experimentation with suitable domestic institutions and agencies and the nurturing of internal economic integration need to be combined with sound macroeconomic policy and some elements of external market integration. This is what economic government is about. The most successful recent cases of development – East Asia, China, India – have managed to find ways of taking advantage of the opportunities offered by world markets – cheaper products, exports, technology and capital – while entrenching domestic incentives for investment and institution-building.

Dani Rodrik has put it succinctly: 'Market incentives, macroeconomic stability, and sound institutions are key to economic development. But these requirements can be generated in a number of different ways – by making the best use of existing capabilities within the context of specific constraints. There is no single model of a successful transition to a high growth path. Each country has to figure out its own investment strategy.'[10]

Development thinking has to shift from a dogged focus on 'market access' to a much wiser and more complex mindset. Developing nations need policy space to exercise institutional innovations that depart from orthodoxies of the World Bank, IMF and World Trade Organization (WTO). In parallel, organizations like the WTO must move their agendas away from a focus on market creation and supervision towards a broader range of policies which encourage different national economic systems to flourish within a fair and equitable rule-based global market order.

The consequence of not encouraging such an approach means that the Washington Consensus bears a heavy burden of responsibility for the remarkable, ongoing resistance to addressing significant areas of market failure. These include:

- the problem of externalities, for example the environmental degradation caused by current forms of economic growth;
- the inadequate development of non-market social factors which alone can provide an effective balance between 'competition' and 'cooperation'; for example, ensuring an adequate supply of essential public goods such as education, effective transportation and sound health care;
- the tendency towards the 'concentration' and 'centralization' of economic life, marked by patterns of oligopoly and monopoly;
- the propensity to 'short-termism' in investment strategy as fund holders and investment bankers operate policies aimed at maximizing immediate income return and dividend results;
- the underemployment or unemployment of productive resources in the context of the demonstrable existence of urgent and unmet needs.

Leaving it to markets on their own to resolve problems of resource generation and allocation will perpetuate many deep-rooted economic and political difficulties. Among them are four:

- the vast asymmetries of life chances within and between nation-states which are a source of considerable conflict;
- the erosion of the economic fortune of some countries in sectors like agriculture and textiles, while these sectors enjoy protection and assistance in others;
- the emergence of global financial flows which can rapidly destabilize national economies;

• the development of serious transnational problems involving the global commons.

Indeed, pushing back the boundaries of state action and weakening governing capacities in order to increase the scope of market forces in a society will mean cutting back on services which have offered protection to the vulnerable. The difficulties faced by the poorest and the least powerful – north, south, east and west – will be worsened not improved. The rise of 'security' issues to the top of the political agenda reflects, in part, the need to contain the outcomes which such policies help provoke.

By weakening the culture and institutions of government and public life – locally, nationally and globally – the Washington Consensus has eroded the capacity of countries around the world to provide urgently needed public goods. It has confused economic freedom with economic effectiveness. Economic freedom is championed at the expense of social justice and environmental sustainability, with long-term damage to both.

Amending the Washington Consensus

The Washington Consensus has come under assault from many sides in recent years, from special domestic lobbies demanding protection for certain economic sectors (agriculture, textiles, steel) to the anti-globalization, environmental and social justice movements. The poor results and performance of the Washington Consensus which I have summarized have invoked deep unease and criticism. Disappointing economic growth and increasing insecurity in many parts of Latin America, economic stagnation or decline in many sub-Saharan countries, the Asian financial crisis and the stark difficulties experienced in some of the transition economies have led to a call to replace or broaden the policy range of the Washington Consensus.

As a result, within the IMF, World Bank and other leading international organizations, there has been an attempt to respond to criticism by broadening the Consensus to encompass the need for state capacity, poverty reduction and social safety nets. Slowly, attention has shifted from an exclusive emphasis on liberalization and privatization to a concern with the institutional underpinnings of successful market activity. A new agenda has emerged which still champions large parts of the old agenda, but adds governance and anti-corruption measures, legal and administrative reform, financial regulation, labour market flexibility and the importance of social safety nets. It can be called 'the augmented Washington Consensus'.

The new emphasis, whose most prominent advocates include Peter Sutherland, founder of the World Trade Organization, is helpful and welcome. But, as Rodrik has emphasized, 'the institutional basis for a market economy is not uniquely determined. There is no single mapping between a well-functioning market and the form of non-market institutions required to sustain it.'[11] The new agenda gives excessive weight to Anglo-American conceptions of the proper type of economic and political institutions such as flexible labour markets and financial regulation. In addition, the whole agenda is shaped by what is thought of as the necessary institutions to ensure external economic integration, such as the introduction of WTO rules and standards.

The new agenda provides no clear guidance on how to prioritize institutional change and gives little recognition to the length of time it has taken to create such developments in countries where it is well advanced. After all, nearly all the industrial countries which have nurtured these reforms did so over very substantial time periods. A more sophisticated, fairer and integrated framework is needed at the international level to address the real needs of the many poorer developing nations, social, economic and political.

Are we moving in this direction? No. Instead a new security agenda geared to the supposed interests of the United States is being deployed. It is to this we must now turn.

3 From the Washington security agenda to a human one

The terrorist attack on the World Trade Center and the Pentagon was a defining moment for the history of today's generations. In response, the US and its major allies could have decided that the most important and effective way to defeat global terrorism and prevent it from becoming a torrent would be to strengthen international law and enhance the role of multilateral institutions. They could have decided it was important that no single power or group should act as judge, jury and executioner. They could have decided that global hotspots like the Israeli/Palestinian conflict which feed global terrorism should be the main priority for coordinated international efforts. They could have decided that the disjuncture between economic globalization and social justice needed more urgent attention, and they could have decided to be tough on terrorism and tough on the conditions which lead people to imagine that al-Qaida and similar groups are agents of justice in the modern world.

Instead they have systematically failed to decide any of these things. Since 9/11, the world has become more polarized, international law has become weaker, and the systematic political failings of the Washington Consensus have been compounded by the triumphs of new Washington security doctrines.

The rush to war against Iraq in 2003 was gravely misconceived. I argued at the time in openDemocracy that it was the wrong war, in the wrong place at the wrong time. Now it can also be seen how globally it gave priority to a narrowly conceived security agenda which is at the heart of the new American doctrine of unilateral and pre-emptive war. This agenda contradicts most of the core tenets of international politics and international agreements since 1945. It throws aside respect for political negotiations among states, as well as the core doctrine of deterrence and stable balance of power relations among major powers. A single country which enjoys military supremacy to an unprecedented extent has decided under its current president to use that supremacy to respond unilaterally to perceived threats (which may be neither actual nor imminent), and that it will brook no rival.

The new doctrine has many serious implications. Among these are a return to the view of international relations as, in the last analysis, a 'war of all against all', in which states rightly pursue their national interests unencumbered by attempts to establish internationally recognized limits (self-defence, collective security) on their ambitions. Once this 'freedom' is granted to the US, why not also to Russia or China, India or Pakistan, North Korea or Iran? It cannot be consistently argued that all states bar one must accept limits on their self-defined goals and that this can be called law. It will not take long for such an approach to become manifestly counterproductive.

Narrow vs broad security agendas

What the world needs is a much broader, indeed global, security agenda that requires three things of governments and international institutions – all currently missing.

First, there must be a commitment to the rule of law and the development of multilateral institutions that can prosecute or validate war when necessary. Civilians of all faiths and nationalities need protection. Terrorists and all those who systematically violate the sanctity of life and human rights must be brought speedily and firmly before an international criminal court system that commands crossnational support and can deliver justice. Internationally sanctioned military action must be developed to arrest suspects, dismantle terrorist networks and deal with aggressive rogue states.

But such action should always be understood as a robust form of international law enforcement, above all as a way, as Mary Kaldor has most clearly put it, of protecting civilians and bringing suspects to trial.[12] Clearly, if justice is to be dispensed impartially so as to ensure international support, no power can act as judge, jury and executioner. What is needed is momentum towards global – not American or Russian or Chinese or British or French – justice. We must act together to sustain and strengthen a world based on common rules to ensure basic human security and protection.

Second, a sustained effort has to be undertaken to generate new forms of global political legitimacy for international institutions involved in security and peacemaking. This must include the condemnation of systematic human rights violations wherever they occur, and the establishment of new forms of political accountability that go well beyond the occasional one-off efforts to create a new momentum for peace and the protection of human rights that have been all too typical of world affairs since 1945.

Third, as already argued, there must be a head-on acknowledgement that the ethical and justice issues posed by the global polarization of wealth, income and power, and with them the huge asymmetries of life chances, cannot be left to markets to resolve. It is not just the case that those who are poorest and most vulnerable, and are linked into geopolitical situations where their claims have been neglected for generations, may provide fertile ground for terrorist recruiters. Terrorism can breed in well-off societies and can be led by middle-class or, as with Osama bin Laden, upper-class figures. But one of the principles of eliminating terrorism has to be to remove those real injustices which terrorists may use, however opportunistically, to further their support and legitimize their methods. For one consequence of globalization of communications is that the experience of injustice in one part of the world can be shared elsewhere.

Of course, terrorist crimes of the kind witnessed on 9/11 and on occasions since (in Chechnya, Indonesia, Saudi Arabia, Pakistan, Morocco and Spain) are in part the work of the deranged and the fanatic and so there can be no guarantee that a more just and institutionally stable world will be peaceful in all respects. But if we turn our back on the project of creating such a world, there will be no hope of ameliorating the social basis of disadvantage experienced in the poorest and most dislocated countries. Gross injustices, linked to a sense of hopelessness, will then feed anger and hostility. Popular support against terrorism depends on convincing people that there is a legal and peaceful way of addressing such grievances. Without this sense of confidence in public institutions and processes, the defeat of terrorism becomes a hugely difficult task, if it can be achieved at all.

Any attempt to develop international law, to enhance the capacity of international institutions for peacekeeping and peacemaking, and to build bridges between economic globalization and the priorities of social justice will itself be threatened by terrorism and the dangers of extensive terrorist networks. But it is also being endangered by the deeply misguided responses to terrorism we are now witnessing. The new security agenda of the American neo-conservatives, alongside the national security doctrine of the current American administration, arrogates to the United States the global role of setting standards, weighing risks, assessing threats and meting out justice. It breaks with the fundamental premises of the post-1945 world order with its commitment to deterrence, stable relations among major powers and the development of multilateral institutions to address common problems.

What needs to be done

Clearly, the issues of security and terrorism are deeply contested. But there are a number of very pressing issues which need to be addressed if we are to salvage the achievements of the post-Holocaust world and build on them in a manner that provides not just security in the narrowest sense (protection from the immediate threat of coercive power and violence), but security in the broadest sense – what I call 'human security' that seeks to ensure protection for all those whose lives are acutely vulnerable.

I have set out how we can go about this in my recent book *Global Covenant*. Here, I will simply list six steps which could be taken to help implement a human security agenda:

- relinking the security and human rights agenda in international law – the two sides of international humanitarian law which together define grave and systematic abuse of human security and well-being, and the minimum conditions required for the development of human agency;
- reforming UN Security Council procedures to improve the specification of, and legitimacy of, armed intervention, with credible threshold tests; linking these to the conditions which would constitute a severe threat

to peace, or to the minimum conditions for the well-being of human agency, sufficient to justify the use of force;

- recognizing the necessity to dislodge and amend the now outmoded 1945 geopolitical settlement as the basis of decision-making in the Security Council, and to extend representation to all regions on a fair and equal footing;

- expanding the remit of the Security Council, or creating a parallel Social and Economic Security Council, to examine and where necessary intervene in the full gamut of human crises – physical, social, biological, environmental – which can threaten human agency;

- founding a World Environmental Organization to promote the implementation of existing environmental agreements and treaties, with a main mission to ensure that the development of world trading and financial systems is compatible with the sustainable use of the world's resources;

- understanding that effective, transparent and accountable global governance requires reliable income streams, from aid to new financial facilities (as proposed by the British finance minister, Gordon Brown) and, in due course, new tax revenues (for example, based on GNP, energy usage or financial market turnover).

Humanitarian armed intervention

I assess how each of these possibilities might be realized in *Global Covenant*. Here, I will consider just one of the more critical issues before turning to how such an overall programme might be achieved. How can we justify humanitarian armed intervention should circumstances so demand? Three compelling accounts have recently acknowledged this question.

First, the report (published in December 2001) of the Canadian-sponsored International Commission on Intervention and State Sovereignty emphasizes the importance of a responsibility to protect people in the face of large-scale loss of life or ethnic cleansing. And it links this responsibility to additional principles which concern the use of proportional means, including last resort use of military power, in the face of severe tests to human well-being, among other considerations.

A second account is offered by Anne-Marie Slaughter. She focuses on three factors which, when present simultaneously, might justify armed humanitarian intervention: possession of weapons of mass destruction; grave and systematic human rights abuses; and aggressive intent with regard to other nations.

Third, Kenneth Roth of Human Rights Watch has argued that humanitarian intervention could be justified if it meets a number of conditions: that it is an intervention of last resort; motivated by humanitarian concerns; guided by, and maximizing, compliance with international humanitarian law; likely to achieve more good than bad; and legitimated via the UN Security Council.

Pressing additional questions arise. These include how one weighs the balance of the different factors involved, how one creates a framework that can be applied to all countries (and not just to those perceived as a threat by the West) and how one creates a new threshold test for the legitimate use of force. All the positions which emerge in this regard need to be tested against the views and judgements of peoples from around the world, and not just against the views of those from the most powerful nation-states, if any new solution is to be durable and legitimate in the long run. This will call for, I argue, a global legal convention.

We need to bear in mind that no modern theory of the nature and scope of the legitimate use of power within a state runs together the roles of judge, jury and executioner. Yet this is precisely what we have allowed to happen in the global order today. We need new bodies at the global level for weighing evidence, making recommendations and testing options. These need to be separate and distinct bodies which embody a separation of powers at the global level.

Because if one is in favour of legitimate humanitarian intervention one also needs to ask who is going to make these decisions and under what conditions. The weight of argument points in favour of taking seriously the necessity to protect peoples under extreme circumstances, and it also points in the direction of amending the institutional structures which pass judgement over these pressing matters. These structures need to be open, accountable and representative. Without suitable reform, our global institutions will forever be burdened by the mantle of partiality and illegitimacy.

4 Towards a new global covenant

At the centre of my argument and proposals is the need to connect the security and human rights agendas and to bring them together into a coherent international framework. To achieve this a global convention is needed to draw up a new covenant for the world. Rather than set out a blueprint of what the results of such a convention should be, it is important to stress the significance of a legitimate process that both reviews the security and human rights sides of international law and also seeks to reconnect them in a global legal framework. This must, in addition, be linked to a larger social and economic framework of global governance, setting fundamental standards for all human life.

One demonstrable result of such an initiative could be new procedures at the UN to specify the set of conditions which would constitute a threat to the peace and the well-being of humankind sufficient to justify the use of force. The question is often put in the form: Do we need to amend the UN Charter to create new triggers for war or armed intervention in the affairs of a country because of its internal policies?

But there is a much greater question which any such convention needs to address. Across the developing or majority world, issues of global justice with respect to government and legal human rights are not regarded as a priority on their own, and are unlikely to be perceived as legitimate concerns, unless they are connected with fundamental humanitarian issues rooted in social and economic well-being, such as basic education, clean water and public hygiene.

In other words, we need to replace the narrow scope and vision of the Washington Consensus with doctrines of a free and fair global economy which also supports a human security agenda. If globalization is to be steered for the benefit of all, the best way to achieve this is by globalizing social democratic concepts and values:

- the rule of law;
- political equality;
- democratic politics;
- social justice;
- social solidarity;
- economic efficiency.

The social democratic balance, past and present

Traditionally, social democrats have sought to deploy the democratic institutions of individual countries on behalf of a particular national project: a compromise between the powers of capital, labour and the state which seeks to encourage the development of market institutions, private property and the pursuit of profit within a regulatory framework that guarantees not just the civil and political liberties of citizens, but also the social conditions necessary for people to enjoy their formal rights.

Social democrats have rightly accepted that markets are central to generating economic well-being, but have recognized that in the absence of appropriate regulation they suffer serious flaws – especially the generation of unwanted risks for their citizens, an unequal distribution of those risks, and the creation of additional negative externalities and corrosive inequalities.

In the build-up to, during and then after the Second World War many Western countries sought to reconcile the efficiency of markets with the values of social community (which markets themselves presuppose) in order to develop and grow. The way the balance was struck took different forms in different countries, reflecting different national political traditions: in the US the New Deal, and in Europe social democracy or the social market economy. Yet however this balance was exactly conceived, governments, as John Ruggie has stressed, played the key role in enacting and managing this programme: moderating the volatility of transaction flows, managing demand levels and providing social investments, safety nets and adjustment assistance.[13]

Although for a few decades after the Second World War it seemed that a satisfactory balance could be achieved between self-government, social solidarity and international economic openness – at least for the majority of Western countries, and for the majority of their citizens – it now appears a balance will be increasingly hard to sustain. Today, the mobility of capital, goods, people, ideas and pollutants increasingly challenges the capacity of individual governments to develop their own social and political compromises within delimited borders. New problems are posed by the increasing divergence between the extensive spatial reach of economic and social activity, and the traditional state-based mechanisms of political control. Moreover, these problems cannot be resolved within the framework of the Washington Consensus, old or new. Equipped with its policies, governance at all levels has too often been simply disarmed or naively reshaped.

Social democracy in a new era

Thus, while the concepts and values of social democracy are of enduring significance, the key challenge today is to elaborate their meaning, and to re-examine the conditions of their entrenchment, against the background of the changing global constellation of politics and economics.

In the current era, social democracy must be defended and elaborated not just at the level of the nation-state, but at regional and global levels as well. The provision of public goods can no longer be equated with state-provided goods alone. Diverse state and non-state actors shape and contribute to their provision – and they need to do so if some of the most profound challenges of globalization are to be met.

Moreover, some core public goods have to be provided regionally and globally if they are to be provided at all. From the establishment of fairer trade rules and financial stability to the fight against hunger and environmental degradation, the emphasis needs to be on finding durable modes of international and transnational cooperation and collaboration.

With this in mind, the project of social democracy has to be reconceived to include five essential goals:

• the promotion of the rule of law at the international level;

- greater transparency, accountability and democracy in global governance;
- a deeper commitment to social justice in the pursuit of a more equitable distribution of life chances;
- the protection and reinvention of community at diverse levels;
- the regulation of the global economy – through public management of global trade and financial flows and engagement of leading stakeholders in corporate governance.

These guiding orientations set apart the politics of what I call 'global social democracy' from both the pursuit of the Washington Consensus and from those who oppose globalization in all its forms.

Social democracy at the level of the nation-state means being tough in pursuit of free markets while insisting on a framework of shared values and common institutional practices. At the global level it means pursuing an economic agenda which calibrates the freeing of markets with poverty reduction programmes and the immediate protection of the vulnerable – north, south, east and west. This agenda must be pursued while ensuring that different countries have the freedom they need to experiment with their own investment strategies and resources within a legal convention that binds states to basic standards.

Economic growth on its own can provide a powerful impetus to the achievement of human development targets. But unmanaged economic development which primarily benefits the already entrenched interests of the global economy will never be geared to prosperity for all. Economic development needs to be conceived as a means to an end, not an end in itself.

Understood accordingly, it should be recognized that while international trade has huge potential for helping the least well-off countries to lift themselves out of poverty, and for enhancing the welfare and well-being of all nation-states, the current rules of global trade, as already indicated, are structured to protect the interests of the well-off against the interests of the poorest countries as well as many middle income ones.

Free trade is an admirable objective for progressives in principle, but it cannot be pursued without attention to the power asymmetries of the global economy and to the poorest in the low and middle income countries who are extremely vulnerable to the initial phasing in of external market integration (especially of capital market liberalization), and who have few resources, if any, to fall back on during times of economic transformation. A similar thing can be said, of course, for many people in wealthier societies. While they are not exposed to the unequal rules, double standards and inequalities of the global economic order in a parallel way to developing countries, if they lose their jobs or have to settle for lower wages, they are also vulnerable in times of major economic shifts.

Any social democratic agenda for free markets must simultaneously address the needs of the vulnerable wherever they are. For the poorest countries this will mean that development policies must be directed to challenge the asymmetries of access to the global market, to ensure the sequencing of global market integration, particularly of capital markets, to experiment with different kinds of investment strategy, to build a robust public sector, to ensure long-term investment in health care, human capital and physical infrastructure, and to develop transparent, accountable political institutions.

In developed countries this will mean the continued enhancement of strong, accountable political institutions to help mediate and manage the economic forces of globalization, and the provision of, among other things, high levels of social protection and supporting safety nets, alongside sustained investment in lifelong learning and skills acquisition. It is striking how seldom this range of policies has been pursued. This seems more a matter of psychology and political choice, and less a matter related to any fundamental obstacles in the nature of the economic organization of human affairs.

5 A global social democratic consensus

A sketch for a social democratic consensus on economic globalization and global economic governance follows. Together with the elements listed above for a human security agenda (see the section on 'What needs to be done' on p. 22), the policies would make a significant contribution to the creation of a level playing-field in the global economy; together, they would help reshape the economic system in a manner that is both free and fair. They include:

- salvaging the Doha trade round, and ensuring a development round that brings serious benefits to the world's poorest countries and to middle income ones;
- reforming the Trade-Related Aspects of Intellectual Property Rights (TRIPS) agreement to ensure it is compatible with public health and welfare, offering flexibility for poor countries to decide when, and in what sectors, they want to use patent protection;
- recognizing that, for many developing countries, phasing in their integration into global markets, and only pursuing this agenda after the necessary domestic political and economic reforms are in place, is far more important than the pursuit of open borders alone;
- building on organizations such as the WTO legal advisory centre, to expand the capacity of developing

countries to engage productively in the institutions of governance of the world economy;

- setting a clear timetable for governments to reach the UN 0.7 per cent of GNP overseas aid target, and raising it to 1 per cent in due course, to ensure the minimum flow of resources for investment in the internal integration of the world's poorest countries;
- supporting substantial further reductions in the international debt burden of heavily indebted poor countries, linking debt cancellation, for instance, to health programmes or to education and the provision of financial incentives for poor children to attend school;
- creating a fair international migration regime that can regulate flows of people in a way that is economically beneficial and socially sustainable for developing as well as developed countries;
- improving cooperation among international financial institutions and other international donors, thus consolidating the development and policy-making efforts of the international community within the UN;
- opening up international financial institutions to enhance the involvement of developing countries by addressing their underrepresentation in existing governance structures, and expanding their role in, among other places, the Financial Stability Forum (FSF) and the Basel Committee on Banking Supervision;
- building global networks and institutions focused on poverty and welfare to act as counterweights and countervailing powers to the market driving international governmental organizations (IGOs) (the WTO, IMF and World Bank);
- instituting a substantial international review of the functioning of the Bretton Woods institutions, created more than fifty years ago, and now operating in an economic context that has drastically changed.

If developed countries especially want swift movement to the establishment of global legal codes that will enhance security and ensure action against the threats of terrorism, then they need to be part of a wider process of reform on these lines that addresses the insecurity of life experienced in developing societies.

Do we have the resources to put such a programme into effect? We may lack the will but it cannot be said that we lack the means. A few telling examples make the point. The UN budget is $1.25 billion plus the necessary finance for peacekeeping per annum. Against this, US citizens spend over $8 billion per annum on cosmetics, $27 billion per annum on confectionery, $70 billion per annum on alcohol and over $560 billion per annum on cars. (All these figures are from the late 1990s and so are likely to be much higher now.) Or take the European Union: its citizens spend $11 billion per annum on ice-cream, $150 billion per annum on cigarettes and alcohol; while the EU and the US together spend over $17 billion per annum on pet food.

What do we require to make a substantial difference to the basic well-being of the world's poorest? Again, statistics are available. Required would be $6 billion per annum on basic education; $9 billion per annum for water and sanitation; $12 billion per annum for the reproductive health of women; and $13 billion per annum for basic health and nutrition. These figures are substantial but, when judged against major consumption expenditure in the US and EU, they are not beyond our reach.

Moreover, if all the OECD agricultural subsidies were removed and spent on the world's poorest peoples this would release some $300 billion per annum. It can be noted that a 0.5 per cent shift in the allocation of global GDP would also release over $300 billion per annum. In addition, a small shift between military and aid budgets (respectively $900 billion a year and $50 billion a year globally) would make a marked difference to the human security agenda. Clearly, the economic resources do exist to put in place reforms to aid the world's poorest and least well-off. The question really is about how we allocate available resources, to whose benefit and to what end. It is not a question of whether there are adequate economic resources, it is a question of how we choose to spend them. We can decide to meet the challenges so clearly facing the world. We know the dangers, the answers are within our grasp.

6 In sum: the argument laid out as a diagram

1 Washington Consensus

Privatization, minimal regulation, free trade and movement of capital, fiscal discipline, flexible exchange rates, secure intellectual property rights

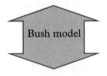

2 Washington security agenda

Order through military dominance, pre-emptive strikes, coalitions of the willing, no binding international human rights laws

3 Social democratic agenda

Strong civil society, state-led investment strategy, strong public sector, priority investment in human and social capital, poverty reduction, developing nations involved at all levels of global governance

4 Human security agenda

Order through (international) law and justice, agreed intervention through UN covenant, protection of all basic human rights

The first box brings out the four elements to the argument: (1) a critique of the Washington Consensus, (2) the way it has now been reinforced by the Washington security agenda, (3) the need to replace the Washington Consensus

The original Washington Consensus	The social democratic agenda: local
• Fiscal discipline • Reorientation of public expenditures • Tax reform • Financial liberalization • Unified and competitive exchange rates • Trade liberalization • Openness to foreign direct investment (FDI) • Privatization • Deregulation • Secure property rights	• Sound macroeconomic policy • Nurturing of political/ legal reform • Creation of robust public sector • State-led economic and investment strategy, enjoying sufficient development space to experiment with different policies • Sequencing of global market integration • Priority investment in human and social capital • Public capital expenditure on infrastructure • Poverty reduction and social safety nets • Strengthening civil society
Washington Consensus (augmented)	**The social democratic agenda: global**
The original list plus: • Legal/political reform • Regulatory institutions • Anti-corruption • Labour market flexibility • WTO agreements • Financial codes and standards • 'Prudent' capital-account opening • Non-intermediate exchange rate regimes • Social safety nets • Poverty reduction	• Salvaging Doha • Cancellation of unsustainable debt • Reform of trade-related intellectual property rights (TRIPS) • Creation of fair regime for transnational migration • Expand negotiating capacity of developing countries at international finance institutions (IFIs) • Increase developing country participation in the running of IFIs • Establish new financial flows and facilities for investment in human capital and internal country integration • Reform of UN system to enhance accountability and effectiveness of poverty reduction, welfare and environmental programmes

The Washington security doctrine	The human security doctrine
1 Hegemonic	1 Multilateralism and common rules
2 Order through dominance	2 Order through law and social justice
3 'Flexible multilateralism' or unilateralism where necessary	3 Enhance multilateral, collective security
4 Pre-emptive and preventive use of force	4 Last resort use of internationally sanctioned force to uphold international humanitarian law
5 Security focus: geopolitical and, secondarily, geo-economic	5 Security focus: relinking security and human rights agendas; protecting all those facing threats to life, whether political, social, economic or environmental
6 Collective organization where pragmatic (UN, Nato), otherwise reliance on US military and political power	6 Strengthen global governance: reform UN Security Council; create Economic and Social Security Council; democratize UN
7 Leadership: the US and its allies	7 Leadership: develop a worldwide dialogue to define new global covenant
8 Aims: making world safe for freedom and democracy; globalizing American rules and justice	8 Aims: making world safe for humanity; global justice and impartial rules

with a global social democratic one, and (4) the need to replace the Washington security agenda with a human security one. It is important to understand that the four elements are distinct. It is possible to advocate a combination of the Washington Consensus and the human security agenda, as a supporter of President Clinton might do. Nonetheless, while the Bush security doctrine only intensifies the negative aspects of the Washington Consensus and is not essential to it, it is unlikely that a social democratic consensus could succeed without the reinforcement of a human security agenda. In the double box on p. 35 and above, the different elements are spelt out in more detail.

2

The Case for Optimism: A Response

Martin Wolf

David Held's flawed, gloomy diagnosis of the global security, trade and policy architecture leads him to faulty conclusions. Martin Wolf, author of Why Globalization Works, *prefers confident realism about the world's future.*

David Held, in his opening chapter, has provided a social democratic agenda for the world. I disagree with it on many levels. But I agree with his favourable view of the potential benefits of economic globalization and admire the ambition and the passion that animates his vision. As I have argued in my recent book *Why Globalization Works,*[1] the intellectually interesting debates about the world's future are among social democrats, liberals and conservatives. David Held has done us a great service by defining the first of those positions clearly.

Nevertheless, I disagree with large parts of his analysis and recommendations. I think Held exaggerates and misrepresents the dangers the world confronts, makes a largely false comparison between the 'Washington Consensus' and US unilateralism in the security field; makes incorrect statements about the consequences of current development policies; and offers suggestion for a new world order that are unfeasible, unnecessary and, in some respects, irrelevant.

A flawed prospectus

David Held's analysis of the dangers the world confronts is deficient. He argues that we risk the potential collapse of the regulation of world trade, are failing to achieve the UN's Millennium Development Goals, are not doing anything about global warming, and are watching the erosion of the multilateral order symbolized by the United Nations. This is mostly wrong.

I agree with David Held on our failure to address global warming, though he ignores the technical and political difficulties that prevent us from tackling it. Renewable energy will not provide the energy we seek, while electorates will not tolerate the huge reductions in energy usage that would deal with global warming in a credible way.

It is wrong to say that there is 'a failure to move towards the United Nations's Millennium Development Goals'. There is such movement, just not fast enough. The proportion of the world's population in extreme poverty is falling, despite the rapid growth of that population. Extreme poverty may disappear from most of Asia in the next two decades. The failure lies largely in sub-Saharan Africa. To describe a shortfall in reaching arbitrary targets in one continent as an element in a 'catastrophic combination of negative factors' seems, at the least, exaggerated.

There is little likelihood of a collapse in the regulation of world trade. The most likely outcome is the postponement of completion of the Doha round. Similar postponements of the completion of negotiating rounds have occurred in each of the last three trade rounds. Trade remains more liberal than ever before. Moreover, many developing countries continue to exploit trading opportunities successfully. China, after all, is now the world's third largest trader. The big failure is in agriculture. The problem here lies not in the international system, but in the recalcitrant protectionism of the rich countries.

Moreover, there has been no erosion of the multilateral order. The World Trade Organization is the most effective international economic institution there has ever been. The United Nations has always been ignored by the great powers when convenient. It has been more effective since the end of the Cold War than at any point prior to then. The International Monetary Fund is weaker today, because its resources are inadequate for contemporary purposes. But, given Held's opinion of the IMF's recommended policies, he should welcome that erosion.

The parallel made by Held between the Washington Consensus and the security strategy of the US is dubious. I fail to see how the Washington security strategy can be described as being against the positive role of governments; it certainly does not wish to abolish the positive role of the American government! More generally, it seeks to ensure that neither hostile states nor terrorists can operate freely against the US. Achieving that aim requires the creation of strong and effective (though friendly) states able to control their territories.

The Washington security strategy is made in Washington. The 'Washington Consensus' is not. It is a label for nothing more exciting than conventional economics. Whether or not the ideas embodied in the Washington Consensus are right, they are widely shared by policy-makers across the world.

A short response to a lengthy argument on development policy is hard, but four further points on David Held's analysis are necessary.

First, when the term 'Washington Consensus' was coined by John Williamson, a centrist economist, its meaning did not include freedom for capital flows.

Second, I know of no evidence that 'one of the key global factors limiting the capacity of the poorest countries is the free movement of capital'. This is hardly surprising, since private capital has shunned these countries almost completely.

Third, the argument that the Washington Consensus prevents developing countries from the development of human capital, economic infrastructure and robust national institutions is wrong. Of course, this is what countries need. But the governments of many of them, particularly the poorest, are incapable of doing any of those things. Neither the Washington Consensus nor 'neoliberalism' has had anything to do with that inability. Far more important are governmental overstretch, lack of resources, misallocation and misdirection of those limited resources (by lavish military spending, for example), pervasive corruption and other forms of malfeasance.

Fourth, it is nonsense to say that cutting back the boundaries of state action must mean restricting services that offer protection to the vulnerable. The opposite is the case. In almost every developing country I know, services provided by the state go disproportionately to benefit middle and upper income groups, not the poor. By cutting back on this largesse, the government could, if it wished, focus its efforts on helping the poor. Of course, depressingly few governments wish to do so.

The Washington Consensus is an imaginary enemy, a bogeyman. The idea that everything would work well with development if developing countries did not have to liberalize or privatize is just wrong.

A misdirected ambition

If David Held's diagnosis is defective, so are his proposed cures. Running through almost all his comments is an unwillingness to confront the fact that sovereignty resides in states that are also of hugely unequal power, competence and wealth. That is why development is such a difficult challenge. That is also why designing a new multilateral security system is a largely idle exercise.

Held assumes that the realities of sovereignty and power can be negotiated out of existence. We can, of course, design any UN Security Council we like. But if the United States government still holds the allegiance of – and provides the finance for – the US armed forces, that council will be a paper institution. The Security Council has to recognize the realities of power. So, of course, does the management of the World Bank or the IMF. Similarly, we can design any development assistance programmes we desire, but a Zimbabwe run by Robert Mugabe will still be driven into ruin and its people impoverished.

Fortunately, such an ambitious reconstruction of the global institutions is unnecessary. Those of us who live in the rich countries can decide to cut protection against agricultural imports or increase aid budgets on our own. We can provide greater assistance to governments in developing countries that are trying to help their people, if we wish to do so. We can intervene to halt humanitarian disasters, such as that in Sudan today, or rescue failed states, should we desire to do so. No one of these things demands a global compact or covenant. All it demands is for the citizens of the rich and powerful countries to insist that their governments act more generously and effectively.

Finally, some of David Held's proposals will not even help achieve the purposes they seek. The construction of a new global geopolitical architecture will certainly not secure development. That depends on what happens on the ground. Aid can help, in the right context. But there are too many cases of failed development in countries with large resource windfalls to be confident that it alone will guarantee success.

Development depends on the ability of countries to exploit market opportunities. Fortunately, if governments do the right things, development will normally happen, as China and now India are showing. Held says that 'unregulated economic development which simply follows the existing rules and entrenched interest of the global economy will not lead to prosperity for all'. Perhaps not. But it would be a huge help.

David Held should cheer up. Yes, the challenges we face are huge. But they are far less frightening than those of four decades ago when nuclear-armed superpowers confronted each other, more than a quarter of humanity lived under totalitarian political regimes and Asia was mired in its millennia-old poverty. Things are getting better. They can get better still. But let us not wait for an entirely implausible and unnecessary reconstruction of the geopolitical order before doing the simple things that will make them so.

3

Delusions of Internationalism

Roger Scruton

David Held's advocacy of global social democracy in response to the world's crises is the wrong answer to real problems, says Roger Scruton.

There is much food for thought in David Held's appeal for a new 'global covenant', and readers will surely be helped by his contribution. We all need to think openly and patiently about the new situation of our world, and about the ways in which we might act together to avert the often discussed, but seldom understood catastrophes. So I am grateful to Held and openDemocracy for making this new approach so widely available.

If I express some reservations – ones that derive from a very different standpoint than Meghnad Desai's below – this is not because I endorse what David Held calls the 'Washington Consensus'; nor is it because I believe that the world can dispense with the kind of global thinking that he has embarked on. It is rather because I believe that there is a hidden premise in his argument that needs to be brought to the surface and examined for its credentials. This is the premise of social democracy itself.

In the days when the labels 'left' and 'right' were accepted moves in political debate, it was common for 'left-wing' writers to confront their 'right-wing' critics with a kind of interrogation: Where are you coming from? The result was to dismiss the critics without listening to their arguments. This meant that debates on the left had a tendency to become internal to the leftist camp, so that fundamental items of doctrine – equality, social justice, internationalism and so on – were never properly examined.

I don't for a moment suggest that David Held is following in that, by now surely discredited, 'left' tradition. Nevertheless, while defining himself in opposition to a supposed 'Washington Consensus', he is assuming a consensus of his own. This assumption is one that I question.

A problem of focus

David Held says that the process of political internationalism (in its current stage of development) began in the immediate aftermath of 'formidable threats to humankind – above all Nazism, fascism and the Holocaust'. Nowhere in his account is there mention of that other formidable threat to humankind, the Communist International, even though its criminal record is a lot longer than those of Nazism or fascism and extends into our own time. Nor is there much awareness of the fact that our new situation is precisely the one brought about by the final collapse of the Soviet Communist Party and of the vast machine of oppression it established and controlled.

Our world is not the post-1945 world that produced the Universal Declaration of Human Rights but the post-1989 world that left the United States the sole remaining superpower, and the country to which all eyes then turned in search of the future.

Held's eyes are also turned in that direction – in my view obsessively so – with the result that the entire global situation is mapped out in terms of an alleged 'Washington

Consensus'. All criticism in his argument seems to be fired in that direction, as though the world would set itself to rights were it not for those self-interested factions at the helm of American government who are determined to bend the world's economy to their own profit.

The version that Held gives of this idea is a sophisticated one, and not everything he says against America is wrong: far from it. But I cannot help thinking that there is a false emphasis here and that the emphasis stems from Held's desire to cling to the social democratic vision, without examining it for what it is worth.

I entirely endorse the criticisms that he and others have made of the World Trade Organization and the near-criminal regime of 'intellectual property rights' which has borne so heavily on third world rural economies. But to imply, as he does, that the impoverishment of the third world countries is a result of the Washington Consensus is to come uncomfortably close to an old and surely dis-credited leftist instinct. Blame Washington, since Washing-ton – alone among the power centres of the world – is responsive to blame.

I am reminded of the way in which so many branches of the 'peace movement', during the years of the Cold War, would direct their fire exclusively at the Western alliance, not necessarily because of a leftist sympathy for the Soviet project, but because of an understandable sense that it is futile to blame governments that permit neither free dis-cussion nor the assumption of blame.

In just this way Held seems to end up blaming Washington for the dire condition of poor countries today – as though Washington were responsible for the Rwandan genocide, for the massacres in the Congo or Sudan, or for the state-propelled environmental disasters in North Korea and China. Are we really to believe that Zimbabwe's transition from a food-exporting to a food-importing country is the result of American trade and foreign policy, and has nothing to do with the fact that Zimbabwe is in the hands of a racist maniac?

If blame is to be allocated, then to direct it all at America, while exonerating the people, policies and leaders of the poorer parts of the world, is to follow a dangerous path. It entails refusing to view people outside the enclaves of Western capitalism as subject to judgement: in other words, refusing to recognize their full humanity.

Three evasions

It seems to me that David Held's argument would look very different seen in the light of three issues that social democrats tend to avoid.

The first is the issue of the free market. Held is right to point out that advocates of free trade and the market economy often lend support to unfair terms of trade. He is right that these unfair terms help to impoverish the countries that are most in need of help. The fault, however, is surely not the market economy, but the subsidies that distort it. Most of these subsidies are hidden: infrastructure, technology, education – all offered at public expense to the citizens of the Western countries, and none available except through immense private efforts in what used to be called the third world.

But how can such impoverishment be rectified? The British empire made an attempt – by building railways and establishing schools, introducing the common law, legal education and access to the highest court of appeal. The expense entailed was calculated (according to 'leftist' orthodoxy) to facilitate the exploitation of the imperial territories, but only (according to the 'rightist' response) in the way that such things are always calculated to facilitate the exploitation of the territories where they are instituted, Britain's own territory included.

The Washington Consensus may be considered a modern equivalent – but the American attempt to introduce economic, legal and political infrastructure into Iraq is immensely controversial in Washington, even among those who have been identified as 'conservatives': witness Francis Fukuyama's article in the *National Interest* (summer 2004).

The attempt is also repudiated by David Held, who yet notes the inadequate provision of essential 'public goods' (including transport systems and education) in the poorer parts of the world. He differs from advocates of the Washington Consensus only in expressing the hope that international institutions, rather than the United States and the economic processes it champions, should take the initiative in providing them.

But this raises a second question: what grounds does Held have for thinking that international institutions would have the slightest interest in doing so? There are powerful arguments, presented by Rosemary Righter and many others, for the view that the United Nations acts not as a judge but as a legitimizer of criminal regimes. It has consistently impeded the essential reform without which its ostentatious parading of human rights and international law is little more than a mask: namely, the introduction of local and territorial rules of law – yes, even in places like Iraq and Syria where such things have not been seen since the tyrants and the secret police took over.

Moreover, in any real emergency, such as the one precipitated by Saddam Hussein's invasion of Kuwait in 1990, the UN depends on the powerful nations to take action, which they will do only if it is in their national interest. In the daily work of global governance the UN acts simply as an unaccountable legislative machine, nurturing a corrupt and overpaid bureaucracy. David Held is understandably reluctant to accept the UN in its present form. But what prescription does he have in mind whereby to reform or replace an institution that is regarded with increasing scepticism by the power on which it principally relies to enforce its edicts?

A third point follows. Held is commendably aware that much of what goes wrong in the world does so because legal order has broken down. What he fails to mention is that international law is without effect in countries which have no rule of law, and treaties of human rights are mere chaff where there are no courts to which the citizen can apply for their enforcement.

The Washington Consensus, he suggests, is in the business of imposing American rules and justice. But American 'rules' are largely the old rules of common law (itself founded on natural justice), and Americans are aware that international jurisdiction will be meaningless without the internal transformations that enable the people themselves to apply it. Their attempt to introduce legal procedures into the legal vacuum created by the Middle Eastern tyrants is surely commendable in itself, whether or not you think that war was the right way to begin it. And you can be against the war in Iraq while recognizing that there is no other way to reintroduce the rule of law.

The problem of equality

Among the many other social democratic assumptions that demand examination is that of social justice itself. Throughout Held's argument there seems to be an implied belief that inequality and injustice are the same idea. If John is rich and Mary is poor, then this is an injustice. But what if John has worked hard while Mary has idled? What if John was born in a fertile place, Mary in a desert? What if John has enjoyed the benefits of a long-standing rule of law, while Mary lives among brigands and nomads?

The root assumption of the social democratic position seems to be that we should work for equality, since without it there can be no justice. But you can make everybody equal – as Stalin did in the Ukraine, or Kim Jong-Il does to North Korea – by taking everything away from all of them. You can enforce equality by confiscating the profits of successful enterprises, however honestly and honourably they have pursued their trade. This conception of equality threatens to lead to a state where the people have nothing and the ruling clique takes what meagre profits there are.

It is undeniable that markets lead to inequality. It is undeniable, too, that there are large-scale imbalances and market failures which ensure that current 'free trade' policies are really no such thing, besides having serious adverse effects on fragile and developing economies. The more naive pronouncements of free market ideologues – many of whom fail to see that the free market is an ideal type with no actual instances – could lend support to Held's conclusion that exclusive reliance on the theory of the market is to jeopardize all the fragile compromises on which humanity has hitherto depended for its periods of equilibrium.

Nevertheless, it must be recognized that a market is not a zero-sum game, in which every benefit achieved by one person imposes a cost on another. Even when constrained by unfair terms of trade, a market, properly conducted, will benefit all participants. Some participants will be rich and others poor, but both rich and poor will be richer than they otherwise might have been. Moreover, there is no injustice in the fact that industrious people have an advantage in the marketplace – just as there is no injustice in the fact that handsome people have an advantage in love or intelligent people in science.

Still, the argument about global governance and the future of humanity is not really about justice, and it seems to me that matters are greatly confused by importing the old question of third world poverty into the new concerns about political order and international security.

It is not poverty but wealth that produced Osama bin Laden, and it is the combination of fossil fuels and fossilized religion that has made Saudi Arabia into the crucible of such implacable embitterment. Underlying Held's vision is the image of America as a country made dangerous by its wealth. However the wealth of America is a result of its democratic politics and common-law inheritance. Unlike the wealth of Saudi Arabia, it is the outward sign of an inner freedom.

The Washington Consensus, as described by Held, stems from a belief that the goal of international relations is not social justice, conceived in social democratic terms as a kind of equality, but social and economic freedom, in which people can obtain a proper reward for their efforts and get the state and the bureaucrats off their back.

Those obsessed with equality will often dismiss the pursuit of freedom as irrelevant or counterproductive, believing, with L. T. Hobhouse, that 'liberty without equality is a name of noble sound and squalid meaning'. That is emphatically not the view of Americans – not even of those Americans (who may well be the majority) who reject Held's 'Washington Consensus'.

American-style freedom, true, is not widely available. But that is because its fundamental precondition (and the precondition of a true market economy) is the rule of law – and because the rule of law has been extinguished all over the world, through no fault of Washington, but on the contrary, despite the best efforts of Washington to insist on it.

I have no solution to the problems that David Held puts before us, yet believe that it is indeed very important to cast one's thought as widely as he does, in order to see the connections that exist between the many problems that beset us. I offer these criticisms, therefore, in a spirit of respectful dialogue.

Nevertheless I am certain that the social democratic consensus assumed by Held is not shared by everyone and is, moreover, largely rejected in the United States – the one country on which, welcome or not as the reality is, everyone depends for positive action. Hence I believe that there can be no new global covenant which is based on assuming such a consensus.

Personally I am more disposed to trust the old global covenant, enshrined in treaties between nation-states. After all, in modern times only nation-states have ever achieved what is most needed, which is a stable and territorial rule of law.

4

The Limits to Globalization: Questions for Held and Wolf

Grahame Thompson

Grahame Thompson enters the debate on the reality and potential of globalization with a dual warning to David Held and Martin Wolf: the international financial system is unsustainable – and its coming crisis may undermine both Held's radical reformism and Wolf's optimistic certainty.

The debate here between David Held and Martin Wolf shows that 'globalization' refuses to die as an issue. Both – and this is true also of other participants in the debate – assume that there are dominant trends in the international system, and this makes possible a serious argument over different policies for its governance.

But it is much more important to argue that the only thing to expect in the international system is the unexpected. There is ample evidence to suggest that what has been happening in the past can quickly and quite radically change. There is no basis on which to think that things will necessarily carry on as before; seemingly deep structures are in fact shallow, apparently fixed dependencies are there to be shattered.

John Maynard Keynes pointed to this essential truth in his *Economic Consequences of the Peace* (1919). He asked: Who would have thought in 1900 that only fourteen years later the world would be plunged into a global confrontation as terrible as the 'great war'?

This observation is surely confirmed by the events of 11 September 2001, to which both David Held and Martin Wolf refer. The issues, then, become how to appreciate this 'unexpected'; how to 'anticipate' it as it were, and how to prepare for radical uncertainties.

How far does globalization go?

There is an important underlying agreement behind the clash of views between David Held and Martin Wolf; that 'globalization' exists. Their debate is over the exact form and consequences of such globalization. Held thinks it needs a reformed social democratic political covenant at the international level to properly establish and codify a legally based cosmopolitan order, while Wolf sees a more benign face to the continuing evolution of existing trends of liberalization and privatization.

For Wolf, the good ship globalization is broadly on the right course, though it might not be going quite as fast as he would like, while for Held the ship needs some serious navigational adjustments to avoid the rocks that for him clearly lie ahead.

To challenge this mutual consensus is difficult. But I would emphasize four things:

- it underestimates the still central role that discrete national economies play in organizing and governing the international economic system (though Wolf does recognize this in part);
- it overemphasizes the development of truly transnational political and economic forces;

- it underplays how 'globalization', such as it is, has over the last forty years mainly involved a 'little dance' between the triad blocs of Europe, North America and East Asia; most of the poorer countries have been left out of the game, as Wolf also recognizes;
- what is emerging in consequence is not so much economic (or any other) globalization but supranational regionalization, driven by ad hoc agreements between essentially still sovereign and autonomous national powers.

Two constraints: labour market and financial system

There are two key structural limitations to the development of a truly global economic system. The first is neglected by Held and Wolf: the labour market. There is no single international labour market in the world and, despite the arguments of Nigel Harris and others in openDemocracy, there will not be one. Rather, the dominant trends are in the opposite direction, towards the restriction of international migration and the attempted relative closure of most international borders to the free flow of labour across them. It is agreed among economists that massive welfare gains could be made at the global economic level if free migration were to be allowed – but it will not be. If anything, the big story over the last forty years has been internal migration from rural to urban areas.

The second, equally important, structural constraint on further internationalization involves the financial system. The existence of competing currencies and financial centres forces a dual disjuncture: between domestic and international economic transactions, and between countries that can borrow internationally in their own currency and those that cannot.

These constraints mean that the international financial system becomes inherently uncertain, so that risks proliferate – hence the increasing demand for ever more detailed, prudential global banking and financial regulation, as well as recurrent crisis management by international bodies. Thus the possibility of a fully coordinated financial system on a global scale further recedes.

These structural constraints are recognized by astute establishment economists who would like to see the US dollar become the single global currency. Indeed, full global financialization can only occur alongside a single global currency and a single recognized central bank; but a moment's reflection is enough to indicate that this is not going to happen, for political reasons if no other. Moreover, the surrogate 'dollarization' of the international system is also not happening to the extent that is often thought – the real story is of a decline in the financial interconnections between the United States and the rest of the world.

The American retreat from globalization

Supranational but regional configurations are a sensible response to the instability of the international financial system. These are being developed by private decision-makers, in respect to trade and financial matters, attempting to organize their international economic transactions with shorter distances in mind, and on a definite regional basis.

It is surprising that Martin Wolf does not mention this trend, since his *Financial Times* column has recently championed the development of an East Asian bond market and an International Monetary Fund-type body for East Asian countries. In any case, the trend is just one indicator of a wider process, one that could – in ways that my late colleague Paul Hirst and I elaborated over several years' joint research – challenge the very notion of globalization itself.

Interestingly, the correlation between the business cycles in the American economy and those of the rest of the world has been declining since the early 1990s – a tendency mirrored by comparable cycles of aggregate investment, employment, productivity and other macroeconomic variables.

In brief, the US economy has, in relation to these indices, become less rather than more 'integrated' with the rest of the world (excluding Canada and Mexico) in the past dozen years; and there is evidence that the same is true (though less intensely) for financial variables also. The existing reality of 'globalization', where it can be said to operate, may have been cooling as a result.

The US was, and remains, preoccupied by its own regional Free Trade Area of the Americas (FTAA) project, designed to consolidate and extend the gains it sees established by the North American Free Trade Agreement (NAFTA) process. This is much more in its interests than another truly multilateral round, and its intentions here are reinforced by the apparently easier task of persuading a small number of regional, neighbouring states to cooperate than that of securing agreement between all 192 WTO parties.

This experience, moreover, will not be forgotten at the global level. The US has resisted supporting any more global negotiating initiatives for new mechanisms of governance (for example, an IMF-led sovereign debt restructuring mechanism or a Global Competition Authority) because of the prospective negotiating difficulties. Better, it calculates, to initiate smaller, regionally based combinations than global ones. Peter Sutherland argued against this trend in his openDemocracy interview,[1] but from the architect of the WTO this could be taken as evidence of its increasing importance.

East Asia and Europe: a future of turmoil?

In this perspective, the changes occurring in the Indian and Chinese economies are not proof that a single globalization is taking place. Even if China's economy continues its rapid growth – and the 'if' is bigger than Wolf might acknowledge – it may try to lead an East Asia-based regional economic system. At present this is constrained by its relationship to the US market, but that too could quickly change.

The US is running an unsustainable balance of payments deficit and an internal budget deficit; China and the rest of East Asia largely finance both in exchange for access to the US market. But for how long can these gross imbalances in the international system continue?

Even without a collapse in confidence in the US economy, at some point there will be a rapid readjustment in the US dollar exchange rate, with unforeseen consequences. If money flows out of the dollar and into sterling, the appreciation of the pound could have profound implications for a highly open economy like Britain's, outside the eurozone and facing the already acute domestic problems of a credit bubble driven by the booming house price market.

The impact of a large-scale readjustment in the dollar exchange rate might also be serious for the eurozone, and the European project more generally, in the wake of the European Union's agreement over its new constitution – which has to be ratified by June 2006 by each of the twenty-five member states. If one of the important European economies decides against the constitution, this could precipitate a more general crisis in Europe and the value of the euro could sharply fall.

Thus, from several directions, the international system is likely to be in greater rather than less turmoil in the short to medium term. Here, David Held's sobriety is more convincing than Martin Wolf's apparent complacency.

Beyond the Washington Consensus

Despite its still tenacious hold over elites who run the institutions of international economic governance, it seems that the Washington Consensus has peaked and is in decline. Its policy programme no longer looks attractive from the viewpoint of those grappling with the actual difficulties of development.

The evidence that the world has entered a post-Washington Consensus era is multiple. Private sector reform, not public sector reform, is top of the new agenda; microeconomic conditions, not macroeconomic ones, are the focus of attention; 'good governance' has replaced non-governance; upgrading and re-regulation are preferred to further privatization and deregulation; self-surveillance and self-monitoring have replaced non-surveillance and pure market solutions. These moves, hesitant though they are, represent a real change in attitude, as David Held acknowledges.

One of the main features of the Washington Consensus approach was an extraordinary, unprecedented emphasis on the integration of economies into the international marketplace – one that almost completely neglected the plight of rural populations, whom it ignored or neglected. Yet cultivating a 'prosperous peasantry' was always a mainstay of a balanced development process. It prevents flight to the urban areas and stimulates a domestically focused integration and balanced growth process. It would be beneficial if the demise of the Washington Consensus allowed space for such considerations to return to the centre of the development agenda.

5

The Far Side of Globalization: David Held's Missing Links

David Mepham

David Held's focus on global and American dimensions of current crises of governance, security and inequality worldwide underplays other significant realities, argues David Mepham.

David Held's essay is a timely, trenchant and wide-ranging analysis of the existing global order. It provides a particularly powerful critique of 'Washington-led neoliberalism and unilateralism' and the extent to which the policies of George W. Bush are damaging the prospects for global security, justice and ecological sustainability.

But Held does far more than this. He frames the debate about justice, legitimacy and governance in a broader philosophical and historical context. His is a persuasive defence of universal human rights, a staunch rejection of narrow nationalism and a strong reaffirmation of the values that motivated the founders of the post-Second World War settlement.

The political challenge that Held poses for today's progressives is also the right one: to develop national and global systems of governance better able to manage our more interdependent world to secure greater social justice, stability, sustainable development and human rights. And he makes a series of strong policy recommendations for doing just that.

National, transnational, global

But despite its ambition and scale, there are three significant gaps in David Held's overall argument.

First, in respect of economic issues – and in his explanation of global poverty and inequality – Held focuses much more attention on reforms to global rather than national governance. It is absolutely the case that unfair global trade rules, tied aid or inappropriate conditionality set by the international financial institutions are damaging to the development prospects of poorer countries. But the destructive policies pursued by some developing country governments are also a key part of the explanation for their economic marginalization and poverty. The current plight of Zimbabwe, for example, is very largely a consequence of the grotesque mismanagement of its economy by the Robert Mugabe dictatorship.

As the New Partnership for Africa's Development (NEPAD) has itself acknowledged, more effective development progress in Africa requires Africans themselves to take more responsibility for their own development strategies, and reform their governance systems to encourage increased economic activity, investment, trade and growth.

A similar point could be made about the economic conditions in many countries of the Middle East. The influential 2002 UN Arab Development Report, written by a group of distinguished Arab scholars, said that 'deeply rooted shortcomings in institutional structures', lack of access to education and weak observance of human rights, especially for women, are a central cause of poverty, inequality and unemployment in the region.

None of this is to suggest that global governance doesn't matter; there is indeed a justified critique of World Bank/ IMF/WTO policy and of the Washington economic consensus, one that David Held makes very well. But alongside this we need a deeper analysis of structures of governance within some developing countries, the extent to which these may hinder rather than advance the interests of poor people living there, and the relationship between external powers and local interests and dynamics.

The second gap in his argument relates to global economic issues, where Held has surprisingly little to say about the role of transnational corporations (TNCs). TNCs are a central driving force behind global economic integration through their production, trade and investment activities. Managed well, these investment flows can bring large development benefits, including to poorer countries. Managed badly, however, inward investment can distort local economies and contribute to human rights violations.

So far, the main way in which companies have addressed these issues has been in the context of their strategies for corporate social responsibility (CSR) – a series of voluntary initiatives to enhance the social impact of corporate policies, on issues such as labour standards, corruption and the environment. But while CSR has brought some benefits, it also has very serious limitations, not least because it is voluntary and there are few penalties for non-compliance.

Many of the most difficult issues surrounding the transnational corporate sector occur in poor countries with weak systems of governance. It is in these circumstances – where local governments are either unable or unwilling properly to regulate the international private sector – that the case for cross-border corporate accountability is at its strongest.

In the longer term, we need a transnational legal and governance framework that applies to companies as well as to governments. In the short term, developed countries

should be urged to use the mechanisms already at their dis-
posal to better hold TNCs to account.

The OECD Guidelines on Multinational Enterprises are
a good example of how this could be done. These contain
a mechanism (reporting through national contact points)
that allows governments to take action against companies
that fall below agreed human rights standards. In October
2002 a UN expert panel on the illegal exploitation of
natural resources in the Democratic Republic of Congo
(DRC), in its report to the UN Security Council, named
over fifty OECD companies as being in breach of the guidelines. However, not a single OECD national or company
has faced any penalty or legal action against them as a consequence of their actions in the DRC. The same is true on
corruption: no successful prosecutions for bribery offences
abroad have been brought under the OECD Convention on
Combating Bribery of Foreign Public Officials of 1997.

The diverse sources of conflict

The third gap in David Held's argument relates to those
roots of conflict that lie beyond Washington's direct
responsibility. He provides a strong critique of what he calls
the 'new Washington security agenda', and he is right to
criticize the misconceived US-led war with Iraq and the
dangers posed by Bush's doctrine of pre-emptive military
action. He is also correct in saying that Bush's policy shows
scant regard for international law and that other countries
will use and abuse the precedent of unilateral action.

But as with economics, so with security, Held appears to
overstate the degree to which the manifold security crises of
today's world can be explained by reference to United States
policy. US policy – under this and previous administrations – has often exacerbated conflicts, through financial

and diplomatic support or arms sales to authoritarian governments or rebel groups. This was particularly true during the Cold War, when both the US and the Soviet Union supported a large number of despotic regimes and proxy armies in various parts of the world. This continues today, although now under the banner of the 'war on terror'. For example, despite its appalling human rights record, Saudi Arabia is a major recipient of US and UK military equipment.

But if the US and other developed countries often make conflicts worse, sometimes very significantly so, their role can also be exaggerated. Not all of the problems of conflict and instability in today's world can be laid at their door. While in the 1990s the US and the UK supported the Mujahideen in Afghanistan – an immoral and foolish policy – the rise of al-Qaida and Islamic extremism cannot be explained merely by reference to this support, or even to US double standards in the Middle East. Developments within the Islamic world and in the Middle East are arguably more important in understanding the rise of this complex phenomenon.

As a general rule, most of today's wars and armed conflicts are taking place in the developing world, within rather than between countries. These often have complex local and regional causes and dynamics. External powers can be significant players, but neighbouring countries are often more so.

Many of these conflicts are rooted in extreme poverty, failures of development and weak governance. The World Bank has described such countries as low income countries under stress (Licus); the UK government now talks of them as countries at risk of instability (Cri). The appropriate policy response towards such countries fits closely with what Held calls the 'broad security agenda' – long-term engagement, a commitment to help build institutions and support development, and a serious attempt to tackle the underlying causes of conflict and terrorism and not merely their symptoms.

In the Middle East, this should mean a much more even-handed approach to the Israeli/Palestinian conflict, helping to reduce the attraction of extremist parties and movements. In Africa and other parts of the developing world, it should mean working with countries to help them build strong and accountable political institutions, in which poor people in particular have a bigger voice. And it should mean identifying those developed country policies – unfair trade rules, tied aid, arms exports – that are damaging to the development prospects of poor countries, and changing them. (IPPR is currently running a research project on this issue, looking at G8 policy towards Africa.)

In exceptional circumstances, a broad security agenda should also include a preparedness to use military force in self-defence or to prevent massive human rights violations. Held refers to the International Commission on Intervention and State Sovereignty (ICISS), whose December 2001 report *The Responsibility to Protect* is a first-class piece of work and the most serious attempt yet to define a set of criteria for intervening in other countries on human rights grounds. Building support for the ideas contained in the report should be a real priority over the next few years.

Progressives have sometimes been guilty of downplaying the importance of hard power in protecting democracy and human rights from those forces that have little or no commitment to either. After the Rwandan genocide such a stance is no longer tenable. But at the same time, progressives need to wrest back the initiative on security policy from the neoconservatives. We cannot tackle conflict, instability and terrorism without a more determined effort to tackle poverty and inequality and the denial of human rights, democracy and justice. David Held's chapter provides an excellent theoretical framework and a radical but practical agenda for doing so.

6

Social Democracy as World Panacea? A Comment on David Held

Meghnad Desai

The development of the world economy has rendered David Held's top-down vision of global social democracy obsolete, says Meghnad Desai.

David Held's opening chapter has already attracted critical responses from Martin Wolf, Roger Scruton, Grahame Thompson and David Mepham. I want to add a sideways comment to this openDemocracy debate, not so much on the details of Held's diagnosis or prescription but on his key underlying assumption.

It is this: David Held pits social democracy as, in effect, the 'good guy' against the Washington Consensus and the Washington Strategy as the 'bad guy'. The ills of the world are to be solved by letting the good guy try his cure; the bad guy is a part of the problem, not the solution.

This is a caricature but it does reflect the ordering assumption of David Held's argument. I don't accept it. In my view, social democracy has itself been in a deep crisis from which it has yet to re-emerge. This crisis is rooted in the fact that social democracy is a political formation appropriate to a certain, historic phase of capitalist development: namely, after the First World War, when the world 'deglobalized' into an archipelago of national capitalisms loosely connected by trade and capital movements.

As I have argued in *Marx's Revenge* (2004),[1] the 1870–1914 world was highly globalized; territorial states exercised only weak control over their economies. In the 1919 to 1980s period, the world deglobalized, thus allowing the territorial state to establish greater control over national economies. This era was characterized also by Fordism, with its large manufacturing units and mass trade unions. When Keynesian economics was added to this mix after 1945, the tragic interwar years were succeeded by the Keynesian 'golden age' of 1945–75. It was in precisely this period that social democratic parties flourished, as Donald Sassoon's *One Hundred Years of Socialism* has shown.[2]

It could not last. From the stagflation of the 1970s onwards, social democracy faced challenges it could not meet. The Fordist economy ended as the unionized working classes fragmented; continued full employment led to a crisis of profitability and consequent outward migration of capital and the decline of manufacturing industry across OECD countries. Public budgets came under pressure and welfare states everywhere became hard to sustain.

The trap of uniformity

The challenge of restructuring Western economies and restoring profitability could only be met by a right-wing, libertarian agenda. To recover its electability, social democracy adopted its enemies' garb, but called it 'triangulation' or the 'third way' to save its own blushes.

The most successful 'social democratic' regimes, like Britain's New Labour or the Clinton presidency, in effect abandoned social democracy in all its essentials. They rebuilt their welfare states around work rather than traditional welfare. Progressive income taxation has been replaced by incentive-based income taxes where most revenue derives from indirect taxes. While the rhetoric is about reducing inequality, poverty elimination is given greater weight in redistributive policies.

This is not a perverse but a logical response to the loss of control of the state over the economy. With unregulated capital movements in the OECD (and even further across the globe), it is not possible for the state to subdue the economy as in the halcyon days of Keynesianism. Rather, the state is subordinate to economic imperatives: capital needs to be retained at home and attracted from abroad, labour needs to be educated and re-educated, and labour markets need to be flexible; budgets have to be balanced, and an open economy is the rule. The social democratic parties which failed to meet such challenges have either faced defeat or been forced to adopt austerity measures, as in France under François Mitterrand.

But the biggest challenge to social democracy has been the issue of the freedom of citizens to access public services. Social democracy thrives on uniformity and allocation from the top; it finds diversity and choice difficult to accommodate. But such institutional approaches in an unequal society lead to unequal outcomes and the perpetuation of inequalities. The prime beneficiaries of programmes of universal provision of health and education are middle-class people who know how to play the system.

Moreover, as modern societies have fragmented and demands are made based on gender, race, ethnicity and age – competing with good old working-class status – social democracy is forced to recognize that statism has its limits. 'Rainbow alliances' must be built to replace unionized, working-class parties. The provision of public services has to become partly private and seeks to accommodate choice and quality.

Social democracy has been most reluctant to decentralize and devolve power since it strongly believes in state control. But states everywhere, not just in the 'third world', are dubious guardians of the human rights of citizens. Civil society, especially in relation to women and ethnic minorities, has had to organize to protect rights and ensure benefits. The effort required for gays to obtain state benefits on the same basis as heterosexuals is one illustration of how oppressive the uniformity of the old welfare state has been.

A post-statist social democracy?

These problems of social democracy also have a global dimension. The problem here is not just that there is no global state, but that even if there were one, it might not be worth having. States do not protect the poor and the property-less; only such people's self-organization has historically done that. The social democratic state imagines itself a protector of the poor, because it was once the protector of the gainfully employed (who might occasionally be unemployed) and eventual retiree. It excluded, until very recently, non-working women and men in informal labour markets.

But the deepest obstacle to the creation of a global order is the sovereignty of territorial nation-states. They show their reluctance to cede or share sovereignty – whether in imposing import tariffs and export subsidies, restricting the free movement of labour by imposing passport and visa restrictions, or violating the human rights of minorities.

States are often reluctant even to comply with treaties they have signed, such as the Universal Declaration of Human Rights. Many practise ethnic cleansing and genocide with impunity. It is when the sovereignty of states has been challenged, ultimately by military power (as in the Balkans, Afghanistan, and indeed Iraq) that regimes grossly in violation of human rights have been removed. Europe's failure to counter such violations in its own backyard and its reliance on United States military power does raise questions about who are the real friends of human rights.

The social democratic programme is engaged in recreating a state at the global level. But this outcome will not necessarily be the sort of state that modern democracies succeeded in creating after a hard struggle over centuries in which ordinary men and women fought for their rights. It will be more like a medieval order within which there will be more than two hundred small and large principalities.

The United Nations itself is built on a principle of inequality via the five permanent members of the Security Council. What is needed is a democratization of the UN through direct representation of 'we, the people' in whose name the UN Charter speaks.

A new global order will eventually be created – but not from a statist, top-down, 'global new deal' type approach. It will be created because in the course of globalization the responses of people moving to where the jobs are and of capital moving to where the profits are will erode national sovereignty. The global order will be created because multinational corporations will demand a uniform standard of environmental or accounting practices in order to operate across the globe.

Indeed such global governance from below could happen faster if individual jurisdictions did not insist on preserving their own laws (as in the European Union). It will require the erosion of state sovereignty and the strengthening of human rights independently of territorial states.

The days when statism was any sort of answer to humanity's problems are past. Certainly not global statism! The social democracy that evolved and decayed in relation to earlier periods of capitalism needs to reinvent itself for the age of globalized capitalism: as a bottom-up, people-centred social movement and philosophy that enables people to solve their own problems by self-organization.

7

The Test of Practice: Global Progress in a World of Sovereignty

Maria Livanos Cattaui

Progress towards a richer and fairer world requires specific, diverse initiatives, practical experiment and patient attention to detail – not high-sounding principles and more international organizations, says Maria Cattaui of the International Chamber of Commerce. In a wide-ranging interview with Anthony Barnett and Caspar Henderson of openDemocracy, she argues that a 'global compact' between business and the United Nations will be more effective than David Held's proposed 'global covenant'.

openDemocracy: What is your view of David Held's argument for a social democratic consensus and a human security agenda to replace the Washington Consensus?

Maria Cattaui: I see nothing new in it. It argues on much the same lines as critics of globalization such as Dani Rodrik or Joseph Stiglitz who are trying to look positive but in reality are rather scared of how economic progress is made. Proposals of this kind are really pie in the sky. Who would govern what David Held calls a 'global covenant'?

Global governance would encounter the same problems as national sovereignty, only more so – that is, accountability, responsibility and building up human capacity to act effectively.

In the case of the global covenant, the challenge would be even greater – because it's unclear who can set themselves up to oversee it. How could they be effective at this level if they cannot, in Held's view, be effective at a national or regional level? I am a sceptic when it comes to any proposal that proposes another international organization as the answer!

As for the issue of security and the linkage between lack of economic progress on the one hand and violence on the other, well, it is pretty obvious. All you have to do is to read Moisés Naím's *Foreign Policy* magazine to see the arguments.

We're all very much aware that there are millions of young people who are unemployed, particularly in high-risk countries across the world, who form the majority of the population, and haven't got a remote chance of ever getting a job. I work on these issues with the Youth Employment Network of the United Nations. We know that one of the things that must be done urgently is to remove the economic, legal and regulatory impediments that many governments and societies impose on their own young people. Angry young people without opportunities are good candidates for extremist and simplistic arguments. The challenge is not only Islamic terrorism. It's also a concern in regions like Latin America. Populism and simplistic solutions can be a real danger.

So, yes, we have to be careful; and I agree with David Held on some of the particular criticisms and recommendations he makes. Of course, I agree that the so-called Washington Consensus is inadequate when taken as a simple recipe. As he says, individually its policies can have merit, but not when applied wholesale. Human beings and economies don't fit into one simple equation. Where I strongly disagree is that there are monolithic answers, or that we need a single alternative approach.

I also want to stress that I don't think that the individual parts of the Washington Consensus should be as easily disposed of as Held suggests. For example, the transfer of assets from the public to the private sector is complex. As I often stress, the transfer of a public monopoly to a private monopoly does not a market economy make! But appropriate and well-prepared transfers of assets can achieve a better, more efficient allocation of capital, with hugely beneficial results.

Each of the elements of the Washington Consensus can be seen as a complex subset that different countries adopt at different rates. For example, tax reform is an extraordinarily powerful instrument to raise revenue if it is implemented correctly. This is particularly important when trade opens up opportunities. Many governments don't take advantage of the benefits that arise by taxing effectively, allocating revenues, creating social support systems and education, or building the infrastructure that's needed (whether 'hard' infrastructure like roads and power systems or 'soft' infrastructure like governmental and regulatory capacity). As I said in an openDemocracy interview in 2001, countries need strong governments if they are to benefit from globalization.

The global compact

openDemocracy: Recently you went to New York to attend meetings on the global compact and the Economic and Social Council (Ecosoc). How do initiatives like these make a difference?

The global compact: ten key principles

Human rights

Principle 1   Businesses should support and respect the protection of internationally proclaimed human
rights; and

Principle 2   make sure that businesses are not complicit in
human rights abuses.

Labour standards

Principle 3   Businesses should uphold the freedom of association and the effective recognition of the right to
collective bargaining; and

Principle 4   the elimination of all forms of forced and com-
pulsory labour;

Principle 5   the effective abolition of child labour;

Principle 6   the elimination of discrimination in respect of
employment and occupation.

Environment

Principle 7   Businesses should support a precautionary
approach to environmental challenges; and

Principle 8   undertake initiatives to promote greater environmental responsibility;

Principle 9   encourage the development and diffusion of
environmentally friendly technologies.

Anti-corruption

Principle 10   Businesses should work against all forms of corruption, including extortion and bribery.

Maria Cattaui: The global compact reflects universal principles that are already agreed by governments. It offers a framework for encouraging practical progress by business and its partners. The compact challenges companies to keep improving their performance in upholding agreed basic principles in their operations around the world, particularly where these are not always properly enforced.

This is where we get down to practical details. The International Chamber of Commerce (ICC) and the UN Conference on Trade and Development (UNCTAD) have set up something called the Investment Advisory Council, an instrument for working with the least developed countries to remove some of the obstacles to investment – not only foreign direct investment (FDI) but, much more important, their own domestic investment.

We're looking at what can be done and in which countries. The steps are not always the same. For example, how do you create business consultative mechanisms, both systemic and systematic, inside some of the new countries in ASEAN (Association of South East Asian Nations)? What are the impediments to setting up new companies? Each has particular problems and there are no universal solutions. Certainly, no big multinational will come in and create 100,000 jobs overnight. It doesn't happen like that.

A good example is Thailand – although it is not actually one of the least developed countries. There the business community worked with the government for a decade on specific legal framework issues – commercial law, changes of the regulatory regime. It took ten years to foster a climate of good governance and accountability that is more friendly towards new business creation. Now we're trying to do the same elsewhere. It's essential to be patient. Real progress – continuous, broad-based steps – can only really be achieved where countries do these things for themselves rather than have them imposed.

The realist route to progress

openDemocracy: You seem to be saying that international organizations and agreements like the global compact are necessary to drive through changes, but that they are not themselves international organizations of governance?

Maria Cattaui: Yes, I see them more as networks for change. Business groups in each country work with governments. They gain and share experience through the approval of entities like the global compact, which provide a process for international consultation and discussion. Implementation needs a wide range of different mechanisms, some ad hoc or experimental. Sometimes a summit is what's needed; or one or two United Nations organizations working on a specific issue; at other times, a regional organization like ASEAN.

openDemocracy: But don't we also need new global initiatives? Take, for example, the contrast between what the rich Western countries spend on military security and their enormous defence industries, as against the huge shortfall in funds to invest in the most basic issues of human security in many developing countries – clean water, education and health. David Held stresses this point, and it was further discussed at a recent conference on the UN High-Level Panel on Threats, Challenges and Change. Some people ask if, for example, Ecosoc could be used to strengthen the voice and opinion of the developing world.

Maria Cattaui: I don't think any one organization is the answer. I am for specificity rather than greater inclusiveness in terms of each agenda. Inclusiveness in terms of geographies, yes; a single overarching agenda, no. It is one of the problems in UN organizations to start meandering, and then duplicate work. Specificity is much better!

On the question of spending on security, I'm a realist. There is no question that military security issues are going to continue to be a concern for many countries. If they are ready to pay large sums in developed countries, that is up to them. That's the decision of the voters in those countries. Most of them are highly sophisticated democracies and it's not my place to comment or tell a country what to do.

The important question is: does military expenditure prevent the rich countries from allocating funds for development? I say it doesn't. I agree that the flows from rich countries to poor countries are highly insufficient. But even if they were increased this would nevertheless not be the answer.

There are other things that the rich Western countries should be doing. Martin Wolf is 100 per cent right in his response to David Held. There has to be progress in the Doha round of world trade talks. We have got to stop this obscene and absurd oversubsidizing and protection of agriculture in rich countries. It doesn't help the consumers in the rich countries. It doesn't help the countries in the global south. It prevents exactly what they need.

The alternative to multilateral negotiations is the bilateral route, where one powerful economy makes a deal with a less powerful one. But these bilaterals will never cover the issues which are of highest interest to the weaker country. They are always discriminatory and will never look seriously at the agricultural problems because the European Union and the United States and Japan will not solve their agricultural conundrum outside the World Trade Organization. I am a huge believer in multilateral approaches to such challenges.

openDemocracy: Peter Sutherland made a similar argument in his January 2004 interview with us.[1] But now he seems to think that the Doha round may be on the brink of failure.

Maria Cattaui: It may indeed. And we should all be very, very worried. Rich countries must continue to improve their offers – but I am afraid that developing countries need to exert leadership and courage to banish rhetoric and also make some better proposals.

Plural solutions in a world of sovereignty

openDemocracy: Is a more open, civil society needed here too? In another openDemocracy interview, Mary Robinson argues that the world is entering a new era of 'citizen's politics' in which people can demand that their national governments implement in practice the principles they have formally agreed to at the international level.[2] Politics still comprises three traditional elements – the citizen, the state and the international – but Mary Robinson sees a shift in the relationship between the elements, with more citizen power. Do you agree?

Maria Cattaui: I look at matters slightly differently than Mary Robinson. The example of China is an illustration. China's joining of the World Trade Organization in December 2001 means that the more progressive components of the Chinese government are able to force the necessary reforms to governance and other structures which WTO membership mandates. This can even be a form of protection, if you wish, to force the pace of domestic reforms.

openDemocracy: But hasn't China been able to win some key concessions to WTO agreements that serve the ends of the ruling Communist Party but not the people of China? For example, hasn't it insisted on derogations regarding labour rights?

Maria Cattaui: The experience of most countries is that the growth of economic capacities internally spurs the very phenomenon that Mary Robinson emphasizes: the rise of citizen demands and citizen responsibility. We see this already taking place in China, albeit in limited ways.

A further example, one that could be in China or India alike, is that rapid economic growth facilitates the appearance of a significant middle class with purchasing power, and with time to articulate social concerns and demands. 'Despite our economic gains,' they say, 'I don't like to walk outside my front door and not be able to breathe the air. I don't like the fact that today I haven't got a social security system that will take care of me in old age or when I'm sick.'

This kind of citizen voice is becoming vocal and notable around the world. Remember: gains stretch. As people reach the economic level that (for example) enables them to take out a mortgage on an apartment, they demand steps that improve overall quality of life. When these demands increase, they can engender a paradox – namely, that the very government that makes improvements in response to them becomes the object of further criticism. But this is the proper, natural process of events: one process pushes another, things don't happen in a linear or purely sequential fashion.

openDemocracy: So would you say, in contrast to David Held, that you see economic citizenship as the basis for political citizenship?

Maria Cattaui: No. It's misleading to say one should come before the other. You need both, often at the same time. But they do reinforce each other. Political or social demands may precede or follow economic progress; but whatever the case, the important thing is to work on the two together.

It is also important to remember that the concept of democracy and its applications in different countries is wildly different. It is not the role of outsiders to say that there is only one kind of citizens' organization, or indeed one kind of economic arrangement. But as progress and accountability enter government, citizens in the countries affected start to make their own kinds of demands on the wider economy, polity and society.

This can be a slow or sudden process; it's never linear. But the more the world opens its markets and stops fearing the displacements and difficulties that can follow, the better. We must take care of the costs of change when we can; but we must stop being afraid of change itself.

My biggest concern is for those countries which are too small, too narrow in their economic base, disadvantaged by geographic location, or surrounded by enemies if they're landlocked or neighbours they don't get on with. There you're dealing with problems that are really intractable.

Sub-Saharan Africa and the Middle East are regions with some of the highest and nastiest barriers to trade among themselves. We have to start right there, on a regional basis, to increase their low levels of trade. ASEAN is an example of how these barriers can be overcome, and we have made progress with the Latin American MERCOSUR countries, which at one stage looked as if they would fall behind.

Existing international organizations can do a lot to help here, in terms of knowledge sharing and technical help. There are also facilities to aid reforms in areas like standardization, customs, and transport. Use them! Let's use what is available now, before we invent new organizations.

We're not yet fully using our existing financial or structural capacity to help countries overcome impediments that are not always of their own making.

So let us multiply the kinds of partnerships that we know already work, and experiment with practical kinds of implementation. We don't need to 'monolithilize' single ideas like David Held's global covenant. For good or ill, we're still working on the basis of sovereignty, with countries and localities wanting as much say as possible in their own destinies. We have to build on this in practical and realistic ways.

8

Top Down or Bottom Up?
A Reply

Patrick Bond

David Held's critique of globalization lacks the toughness and radicalism required to generate the understanding and politics that the world's people need, says South Africa-based scholar and global justice campaigner Patrick Bond.

To offer a critique of David Held's chapter – especially in isolation from the book in which its argument is more fully elaborated – carries two risks: both of not doing the argument justice, and of making conceptual distinctions with potential allies, of sharpening the lines of difference for the sake of clarity, maybe beyond the point of comradeship.

But David Held runs even greater risks by abbreviating his imaginative work on cosmopolitan democracy[1] (which emphasizes process, something his chapter above omits), and by emasculating the chapter's twin core themes, 'dangers' and 'answers'. As a result, I fear he isn't yet genuinely engaging the passions, analytical perspectives and concrete programmes of radical global justice activists. I suspect that the anti-capitalist comrades in Johannesburg from where I write, for example, will have fundamental disagreements with Held on a range of issues: analysis, strategy, organizational orientation, alliances and tactics.

It may be that Held gives a low priority to addressing this more radical audience, but the points of divergence with it are still important to debate because of their substance. Three are worth highlighting here:

- the importance of a tougher, deeper critique;
- the need to avoid what I call 'reformist reformism' – reforms that do not challenge economic, social and political structures that reproduce inequality, but which actually reinforce them;
- the opportunities for a more radical, 'non-reformist reform' strategy based on principles and scale politics – that we can summarize as 'decommodification' and 'deglobalization'.

What is the danger?

There are multiple dangers in any political strategy. But for many of us who have experienced a 'liberated' South Africa during these past ten years, when income distribution in the world's already most unequal society actually worsened, the most serious is that 'reformist reforms' of neoliberal capitalism amplify the adverse consequences of both 'globalization' and 'global governance'.

From a growing literature of political-economic work arguing this case more fully than space here permits, there are three critiques of David Held's approach.

First, isn't the dramatic rise of globalization actually a function of what might be termed 'capitalist crisis'? Robert Brenner, Robert Pollin, John Bellamy Foster, Ellen Meiksins Wood, Robert Biel and Harry Shutt, among others, provide conceptual underpinnings and updated empirical accounts of sustained crisis tendencies in the world economy's core regions.[2]

The symptoms of these tendencies include:

- three decades of lower GDP growth (indeed, negative per capita GDP if we factor in pollution and exhaustion of non-renewable resources);
- a much lower rate of profit on productive activity;
- consequently untenable financialization (where returns are much higher) and periodic financial collapses;
- frantic outsourcing of production across the world and hyperactive trade;
- the emergence of system-threatening ecological problems;
- soaring inequality; and
- a near-universal reduction in workers' remuneration and in the social wage.

All of these symptoms are associated with the neoliberal project during a period of persistent capitalist overaccumulation.

Second, in order to displace rather than resolve the crisis, the response of capitalism in its imperialist phase is to amplify combined and uneven development. David Harvey, drawing on Rosa Luxemburg's insights into the interactions between capitalism and non-capitalist eco-social processes, explains how the permanent process of primitive accumulation evolves into what he terms a system of 'accumulation by dispossession'. The system updates and deepens traditional problems, including (in his words):

- commodification and privatization of land and the forceful expulsion of peasant populations;
- conversion of various forms of property rights (common, collective, state) into exclusive private property rights;
- suppression of rights to the commons;
- commodification of labour power and the suppression of alternative (indigenous) forms of production and consumption;

- colonial, neocolonial and imperial processes of appropriation of assets (including natural resources);
- monetization of exchange and taxation (particularly of land);
- slave trade;
- usury, the national debt and ultimately the credit system as radical means of primitive accumulation.

Accumulation by dispossession intensifies with the onset of capitalist crisis and the widespread adoption of neoliberalism by political elites, as the system seeks to mitigate and displace (though never fully resolve) crisis tendencies. Harvey interprets these as 'spatial and temporal fixes' for overaccumulated capital, which in turn serve as crisis management tools.[3]

Hence, the sphere of reproduction – where much primitive accumulation occurs through unequal gender power relations – remains central to capitalism's looting, particularly in areas (like Johannesburg) characterized by migrant labour flows. This labour is cheap thanks in part to the superexploitation of women (in childrearing, health care and elder care) which replaces advanced capitalism's state-supplied (or in the US, firm-based) schooling, medical aids and pension schemes.

This neoliberal agenda represents not merely 'too narrow a set of policies to help create sustained growth and equitable development', as Held quaintly puts it. Rather, the core point of neoliberalism is to restructure ecological-social-economic relations in fundamental ways, in the interests of capital.

Research by Isabella Bakker, Stephen Gill and their colleagues shows how reprivatization of social reproduction involves at least four shifts in social institutions and livelihood, particularly in poorer countries:

- household and caring activities are increasingly provided through the market and are thus exposed to the movement of money;
- societies seem to become redefined as collections of individuals (or at best collections of families), particularly when the state retreats from universal social protection;
- accumulation patterns become premised on connected control over wider areas of social life and thus on provisions for social reproduction;
- survival and livelihood become more pressing, with a large proportion of the world's population having no effective health insurance or even basic care.[4]

Third, Leo Panitch and Sam Gindin (among others) have anatomized the power and centrality of Washington to the management of empire: in the form of the neoconservative petro-military-industrial complex in the Bush White House and Pentagon, and of the 'Washington Consensus' nexus of the US Treasury, Bretton Woods institutions and Wall Street.[5] The fusion of global justice activism and anti-war protest has exposed these two sides of the Washington coin (and if Held wanted to apply the same spirit of critique to the earlier epoch of global-institutional restructuring, an understanding of the same themes would also be helpful).[6]

In sum, the dangers Held highlights aren't a 'crisis of globalization' but of world capitalism. By adjusting the analysis, a different sense of strategy emerges.

Where are the answers?

If David Held's assessment of the 'dangers' is misconceived, his 'answers' also disappoint, because the overarching global governance agenda is already off the mark.

'Without suitable reform', he writes, 'our global institutions will forever be burdened by the mantle of partiality and illegitimacy.' But these are not 'our' institutions – they are the tools of global capital and the petro-militarists in the White House and Pentagon. In any case, suitable reforms have proven impossible, given the terribly adverse global-scale balance of forces prevailing in recent years, and for the foreseeable future. Hence, virtually all feasible global-scale reforms actually legitimize, strengthen and extend the system of accumulation by dispossession.

The radical activist community perceives the need to see the displacement of the crisis into the wider institutional and social spheres outlined above as a challenge to be fought, not conceded at the outset. This can be seen in two areas.

First, the institutional rearrangements and slightly more serious post-Washington policy adjustment promoted by Held have already done far more harm than good, especially since the aim of the world's rulers thus far has been to 'augment' not transcend neoliberalism. (Held seems grudgingly to admit this in his albeit unnecessary defence of John Williamson.) In this light, Held's worries – about the potential collapse of the regulation of world trade in such a way that it will worsen not redress global inequality; the failure to meet the United Nations's Millennium Development Goals (MDGs); worsening global warming in the absence of the Kyoto protocol's implementation; or the Bush regime's 'systematic attack on the multilateral order' – are misconceived. In short, reformist reforms don't – and can't – work if the objective is to solve the problems, not stabilize the system.

Second, under these circumstances, the radical activist community will continue to find ideas like 'humanitarian interventionism' – what Held calls 'the Washington security consensus' – fatally flawed. Instead, for strategic and alliance purposes, we need a far more serious anti-imperialism than Held offers – an approach that can raise the costs of belligerence to the Washington-London-Canberra-Rome-Warsaw nexus, and that does not merely channel the next US President's aggression through the multilateral bureaucracies. After all, the UN has proven persistently useless and indeed collaborative in settings like Iraq, notwithstanding Kofi Annan's recent pronouncement on the illegality of the war.

The problems that Held identifies are indeed crucial, but the perspective from which he approaches them concedes too much. For example, Held fails to make the case for alleged 'reforms' of the World Trade Organization within the 'Doha development agenda' (a euphemism for liberalization, as Robert Wade has pointed out). The radical internationalist flank of the global justice movements, as well as most 'third world' nationalists (of both progressive and authoritarian tendencies), were thrilled when the Cancún summit failed; unlike Held, they did not see Doha as a step forward, nor bilateral trade agreements as the only alternative to the WTO.

Indeed, Held is on very weak ground (with Geoffrey Garrett and Jagdish Bhagwati) in attempting to distinguish 'good' trade liberalization from 'bad' financial liberalization. He should take more seriously the countervailing ideas of Walden Bello, Vandana Shiva, Jayati Ghosh, Lori Wallach and especially Ha-Joon Chang and Ilene Grabel.[7]

Held worries that because of the Cancún breakdown, there is a real danger that the Doha trade round will collapse – or produce derisory results. No: a further collapse would have been preferable, given the awful renewed WTO framework established in Geneva in the autumn of 2004, notwithstanding some rhetorical (not yet real) agricultural subsidy cuts.

Held regards the millennium development goals as 'the moral consciousness of the international community'. It was, though, the elite United Nations which generated (non-transparently) the MDGs, at the same time as the organization moved to embrace the so-called Washington Consensus with its pro–corporate global compact, its endorsement of 'Type 2' (public–private partnership) privatization strategies, and its collaboration with the World Bank. In any case, the bogus 2015 targets are far less important than the actual social struggles underway across the world for basic needs and democracy. An obsession with MDGs is a diversion from solidarity with the real agents of development history.

Held is absolutely correct that 'there may have been no point in setting these targets at all, so far are we from attaining them in many parts of the world' – but this is also because the institutions which set the goals are so far from the people who need to own the struggles and their victories. As for a 'sustainable framework for the management of global warming', Kyoto definitely is not the answer – as Carbon Trade Watch, CornerHouse and the TransNational Institute demonstrate.[8]

Held is right that the world needs 'social democratic globalization and a human security agenda'. The big questions are: how, what and when? But if (as in Held's opening chapter) the 'how' – by which I mean the process, not the top-down reform idea – is wholly ignored, then the balance of forces associated with winning reforms may lead to a regressive 'what': a pale twentieth-century definition of social democracy that merely polishes capitalism's roughest edges as a gambit to artificially (and unsustainably) keep it looking fresh on the outside, well beyond its expiry date.

Instead, the task now is to inspire our progressive movements to remake globalization from below, through deglobalizing capital and intensifying international solidarity in spheres where people are struggling against accumulation by dispossession.

The third question, 'when', is also crucial; for without

showing how to change the balance of forces, Held's strategy could entail prematurely putting in place new institutional forms which could exacerbate, not resolve, the crisis.
Hence many activists celebrate what Held laments: that
'the value of the UN system has been called into question,
the legitimacy of the Security Council has been challenged,
and the working practices of multilateral institutions have
been eroded'.

Indeed, given the power structures, the militarism and
the neoliberal processes that are continually reinforced
in the UN, why not let it instead (as Tariq Ali advocates)
'go the way of the League of Nations'? That would leave
two other possible approaches at this present stage, ahead
of a future global governance system when conditions are
more amenable: decommodification and deglobalization.

Bridges to the future: deglobalize, decommodify

The strategic formula implied by 'deglobalization' does not
imply the revival either of autarchy (as in the former Albania
or current Burma or North Korea), of corrupt 'third world'
chaos (contemporary Zimbabwe), or of authoritarianism
(Malaysia).[9] Instead, movements like the South African
independent left articulate it in a way that combines internationalism with demands upon the national state to 'lock
capital down'. This could begin, as an example of what must
be done, by removing the boot of the Bretton Woods institutions from the necks of the poor in the global south. The
World Bank Bonds Boycott is having remarkable success in
defunding the institution that is in the vanguard of international neoliberal repression.

In addition, South African and other activists have won
dramatic victories in deglobalizing the Trade-Related
Aspects of Intellectual Property Rights (TRIPS) regime,

by demanding generic anti-retroviral medicines instead of branded, monopoly-patented drugs. Similar struggles are underway to deglobalize food, especially given the genetically modified organisms threat from transnational corporations, to halt biopiracy, and to expel the water and energy privatizers.

These are typically 'non-reformist reforms' in so far as they achieve concrete goals and simultaneously link movements, enhance consciousness, develop the issues and build democratic organizational forms and momentum.

This is a matter for nuanced scale politics: determining whether local community, subnational, national or regional strategies can best mitigate and reverse global economic tyranny for particular issues. To his credit, Held does endorse the central deglobalization strategy, favouring 'internal economic integration – the development of [a society's] human capital, of its economic infrastructure and of robust national market institutions, and the replacement of imports with national production where feasible'. But does he not see that his emphasis on legitimating and strengthening the WTO, and extending its range, will make that strategy even harder to pursue than it is today?

The main reason to deglobalize is to gain space to fight neoliberal commodification. The South African decommodification agenda entails struggles to turn basic needs into genuine human rights, including:

- free anti-retroviral medicines to fight Aids (hence disempowering Big Pharma);
- 50 litres of free water per person per day (hence ridding Africa of Suez and other water privatizers);
- 1 kilowatt hour of free electricity for each individual every day (hence reorienting energy resources from export-oriented mining and smelting, to basic-needs consumption);

- extensive land reform (hence de-emphasizing cash-cropping and export-oriented plantations);
- prohibitions on service disconnections and evictions;
- free education (hence halting the General Agreement on Trade in Services); and a
- free 'basic income grant' allowance of $15 per month (advocated by churches, NGOs and trade unions).

All such services should be universal (open to all, independent of income levels), and (where feasible) financed through higher prices that penalize luxury consumption. This potentially unifying agenda could serve as a basis for large-scale social change, in the manner that Gøsta Esping-Andersen has discussed with respect to Scandinavian social policy.[10] In most of the campaigns above, substantial concrete victories have already been won, and sophisticated mobilizations have taken the struggles forward.

David Held is right to argue that 'while the concepts and values of social democracy are of enduring significance, the key challenge today is to elaborate their meaning, and to re-examine the conditions of their entrenchment, against the background of the changing global constellation of politics and economics'. Today, it is the world's radical activists, especially in the new social movements springing up across the global south, who are addressing that challenge most seriously. It really behoves a great thinker like Held to seriously engage with and endorse the social democratic agenda where it is emerging and where it offers hope of advance: from the bottom up.

9

Global Governance from Below

Benjamin Barber

Barber calls for an account of political change rooted in the realities of global interdependence. He is critical of what he takes to be Held's reliance on normative solutions that are ethically unimpeachable but practically unrealizable.

David Held's diagnosis of the dangers arising out of the Washington Consensus and the Washington security agenda for democratic globalization is astute and compelling. Like Kant, however, Held relies on normative solutions that are as ethically unimpeachable as they are practically unrealizable. I want to underwrite his goals looking to a new global covenant rooted in the rule of law, political equality, democratic social justice, social solidarity and economic efficiency, but offer a somewhat different (if not incompatible) framework for considering their realization rooted in the realities of interdependence.

In Kant's time, as the nation-state was strengthening its hold on the political imagination of Europe and the idea of democratic sovereignty was emerging as a key organizing concept for collective life, seekers of global comity faced a Hobbesian dilemma: the social contract that secured peace and justice within societies was establishing a state of nature among societies in which the 'war of all against all' depicted by Hobbes prevailed. Advocates of a global order were left with a normative discourse urging global peace that was contradictory to Hobbes's most trenchant observation: that 'covenants without the sword' – agreements without enforcement – are of no use to men in settling conflicts or securing justice. It was no different in international affairs.

The modern debate about international cooperation and global democracy remains to some degree mired in this dilemma. Normative appeals are rooted in the 'could/would/should' normative mode where what 'must' happen carries the burden of argument. David Held introduces a worthy agenda under his project on social democracy with language insisting the agenda 'must be pursued while ensuring that different countries have the freedom they need to experiment . . .' He urges us to accept that 'the project of social democracy has to be reconceived to include five essential goals'.

I will reframe the democratic globalization project first of all by redescribing the setting for the debate. I will then focus on what I believe is the real impediment to realizing a global democratic agenda: the persistence of national state sovereignty and the absence of any convincing form of global sovereignty. In the absence of a global sword, no appeal to global governance or international democratic institutions – whether top down or bottom up – is likely to have the teeth to enforce its goals, whether they are to stave off global terror or secure global peace and justice.

The context of interdependence

Held cites Kant observing that we live 'side by side'. But in the eighteenth century 'side by side' suggested proximity in villages, municipalities, provinces and to a limited degree in new nation-states. Although side by side might be stretched to imply some more encompassingly abstract, cosmopolitan human coexistence, it could not possibly have entailed what today is the actual side-by-side existence of women and men the world over in global virtual space in arenas defined by ecological, economic, technological and market interdependence. For all practical purposes most of what happened to people several hundred years ago was local, and much of what happened was not political at all – a function of families and neighbourhoods rather than of kingdoms and republics. The reality of human life today is interdependence. Lives are intertwined in ways that, though often invisible, conjure a global web of cause and effect and that give to almost every individual action an economic or political resonance that impacts others across the globe. For the most part it is a blunt and brutal, even malevolent, interdependence that is at stake, one defined by global health plagues, environmental disasters, international crime, the worldwide drug trade, the proliferation of weapons of mass destruction, predatory global markets and of course terrorism. Tsunamis do not carry a passport; Aids doesn't stop for customs inspections; technology knows no frontiers; and it is not just doctors who operate without borders in this brave new world, but child prostitutes, mercenaries, migratory labourers, financial capitalists, disease-bearing travellers and stateless terrorists.

Our reality then is interdependence. Full stop. I am not advancing a theory about how things should be or might be. Only a description of the way things actually are. I will not argue nations ought to think beyond their own borders, but observe the borders defined by their sovereignty no longer wall off the world as they once did. The French kid who wakes up in Lyon, like the American kid in Chicago and the Lebanese kid in Beirut and the Japanese kid in Kyoto, wakes up in a world that faces common threats, common diseases, common dangers and common plagues and also shares common culture, common brands and common goods. Chicken pox and measles, parochial diseases of insular societies, have been pushed aside by HIV and SARS, global epidemics born in distant lands but made a threat to people everywhere because technology, transportation and communications move millions of people across traditional boundaries and frontiers that can no longer insulate peoples from one another. Residents of Long Island worry nowadays not about the West Hampton virus but about the West Nile virus. Brooklyn bloggers log on to the world wide web, not the Verrazanno Narrows web. Overheated New Yorkers worry not about Manhattan warming but about global warming. Tropical deforestation in Brazil and Indonesia impact Japan and Canada and make warming a global problem that no single nation or government, however ecological minded it might be, can deal with by itself. Tsumanis impact several continents at once, while rising seas can inundate hundreds of millions of coastal towns and cities around the world. Images and information travel the planet on an electronic highway without customs barriers, so that we can no longer distinguish American or French or Indian or Japanese forms of entertainment or news or knowledge from one another, even where America may still dominate the knowledge industry (hardware and software alike), because American companies are no longer really American. Computers, digitized data transmission and satellites along with the sophisticated software programs that drive them and the global-conglomerate-owned news and entertainment content that constitute their meaning comprise a communications nexus that is truly global and states can do little to control content or its distribution.

This is the challenge of actual interdependence and is a far cry from Kant's polite abstractions. Yet, while real, interdependence is often hard to discern. Prior to realizing projects for normative interdependence organized around a new international agenda, a more encompassing consciousness of the realities of interdependence will be necessary. Hence the importance of reframing the challenge of global governance in the compelling language of actual interdependence. Once the realities of interdependence are acknowledged, the task of global governance in the face of persistent sovereignty is clearer. Nineteenth-century political institutions organized around sovereign independence, national society and a world of sovereign nations face twenty-first-century challenges premised on transnational problems and global challenges. Political philosophies rooted in independence face realities rooted in interdependence.

The persistence of sovereignty and the need for a global sword

The challenge is clear: not simply to overcome sovereignty and its often atavistic imperatives but to recognize it has already been fatally compromised in key arenas. Not to urge normative ideals to overcome 'sovereigntist' realities, but to recognize post-sovereigntist realities in reaching for and securing global institutions; to find a foundation in global institutions not merely for cooperation but for enforcing the mandates yielded by such cooperation. To resolve the Hobbesian dilemma in an era of interdependence by forging a global sword capable of enforcing global covenants. The alternatives we face are not the realism of ongoing sovereignty or an idealistic appeal to global governance; they are a starker choice between global governance or global anarchy. Preserving absolute sovereignty in some nineteenth-century form is simply not on the table.

There is thus more than a little irony in the fact that while sovereignty remains the first principle of international affairs for the United States, its reality has already been fatally compromised by the brute facts of interdependence. In his second inaugural address, President Bush wisely observed that 'the survival of liberty in our land is increasingly dependent on the success of liberty in other lands'. Yet this recognition of interdependence is often contradicted by American action in the world. Thus, even as the United States refuses to place its troops under foreign commanders and promulgates a preventive war doctrine that gives it the sovereign right to decide when and where and against whom it will wage war, it suffers from an ever weakening sovereignty in other key areas. Despite its global economic hegemony, Washington can no longer prevent a single job or factory or company from leaving the United States for more profitable venues elsewhere, cannot stop alien viruses from entering its territory, cannot control financial capital, cannot prevent intellectual piracy on the internet. Sovereignty remains a powerful word and the justification for a great deal of what nations do today, but as a reality it has lost much of its potency. Terrorism, like all international crime, testifies to the insufficiencies of sovereignty. The United States could protect neither the capital of finance at the World Trade Center nor the headquarters of its vaunted military machine at the Pentagon, despite the fact that the 'invading force' was armed only with box cutters and fanatic zeal. Indeed, the hijackers came from inside the US, not outside, and the 'states that harboured them' prior to the attack were not Afghanistan and Iraq but New Jersey and Florida.

What is true for the hegemonic hyperpower that is the United States is even more true for less powerful nations. All sovereign states, including those that have just recently struggled for or achieved national liberation and novel independence, face forces impossible to regulate or control through unilateral sovereign action. So that while states still live in the shadow of the idea of independence, they are learning the hard way that there is neither freedom nor equality nor safety from tyranny nor security from terror on the basis of independence alone. That in a world in which ecology, public health, markets, technology and war affect everyone equally, interdependence is a stark reality upon which the survival of the human race depends. That where fear rules, and terrorism is met by 'shock and awe' only, neither peace nor democracy can ensue. That while we have yet to construct those global institutions that might offer us a benevolent interdependence, we are beset by global entities that impose on us the costs of a malevolent and often anarchic interdependence. That in the absence of a new journey to democratize our interdependence, we may lose the blessings conferred by the old journey to democratic independence.

Where once nations depended on sovereignty alone to secure their destinies, today they depend on one another. In a world where the poverty of some imperils the wealth of others, where none are safer than the least safe, multilateralism is not a stratagem of idealists but a realist necessity. The lesson of 9/11 was not that rogue states could be unilaterally pre-empted and vanquished by a sovereign United States, but that sovereignty was a chimera. HIV and global warming and international trade and nuclear proliferation and transnational crime and predatory capital had already stolen from America the substance of its cherished sovereignty well before the terrorists displayed their murderous contempt for it on that fateful morning.

Although America still seems to prefer to play the Lone Ranger – or Gary Cooper in the film *High Noon*, where the sheriff must take on four desperados all by himself – the facts of interdependence require global posses, communities working together, to tame the anarchy of global reality. To take the most obvious example, terrorists are not nations, which is why even a successful war against rogue nations cannot overcome and has not defeated terrorism. Whether or not they are supported by rogue states, terrorist groups are in effect malevolent NGOs that operate in the interstices of the international system. Like virulent parasites that live in the bellies of wild beasts, when their hosts are slain they simply move on to occupy other beasts. Al-Qaida did not die when the Taliban were defeated, they moved on to Indonesia and over to Pakistan and on to Sudan and Saudi Arabia and into Iraq, and back to Buffalo, New York and Miami, Florida where they had been before 9/11! They use the new transnational networks of finance, telecommunications, transportation and trade to do their business across national borders. If the states that confront them cannot use international tools at least as effectively as the terrorists use them, there is little hope that terrorism will be overcome.

Yet while international cooperation is desirable and necessary, it is clear that the obstacles that still stand before those who seek new institutions of global governance are as various as they are intractable. The refusal of the United States under the Bush administration to negotiate an understanding that might allow it to sign the Land Mines Treaty (already signed by over 140 nations) is an example. The United States has good reasons to expect the treaty signatories to recognize its special responsibilities as a global policeman and the role mines can play in protecting thinly deployed troops (as in South Korea). But by the same token the United States has an obligation to work hard to draft a treaty it is able to sign. Some of the same problems face the new International Criminal Court. The United States believes with some justification that this new institution could end up as a kangaroo court for troops it deploys on behalf of UN or other peacekeeping missions (although the court's jurisdiction begins only where nations fail to bring their own citizens to justice). But the imperatives of interdependence call for negotiations that allow the United States to join under reasonable conditions rather than obstinate American unilateralism or obstinate international high-mindedness that chooses hypocritically to overlook the United States's special responsibilities.

In other words, whether it is the Land Mines Treaty or the Criminal Court or other obligations such as the Kyoto Treaty on Global Warming or the anti-ballistic missile treaty, or the Law of the Sea Treaty, the current atmosphere makes the United States a stubborn loner and its international interlocutors ineffective suitors for American cooperation. The battle in the United Nations prior to the war in Iraq was typical of an America too anxious to act without multilateral cooperation and a United Nations afraid to act at all. Yet this is in part because sovereignty remains the first principle of the United Nations. It is a congress of nations and, the Secretary-General's Office notwithstanding, represents those nations rather than the people of the world. It is not a 'we the people' organization but a 'we the nations that represent peoples' organization. It embraces the sovereignty that stands in the way of its effective international work. Thus, while it is true that the United States has been quick to play the sovereignty card, so too have other nations when their vital interests are at stake or where they believe their interests are better advanced outside than inside the General Assembly. Nor is America's recent critic 'old Europe' (in Secretary of Defense Rumsfeld's dismissive phrase) itself free of blame for obstructing international cooperation. Its hypocritical support of agricultural and cultural subsidies for its own challenged economic sectors despite its putative adherence to free trade doctrines even as it prevents the third world from protecting its own vulnerable agricultural sector is evidence of this hypocrisy, which destroyed the trade talks at Cancún in the autumn of 2003.

Yet the primary challenge remains that of Hobbes: that a recognition of the realities of interdependence can mean nothing more than an acknowledgement of a global anarchy that cannot be controlled; that a devotion to cooperation and global comity can be nothing more than an empty formula that cripples individual nations without offering enforceable global solutions. The United States may be wrong in thinking it can and should do itself what a united coalition of nations cannot or will not do, but it is right to argue that true global governance in the name of democracy and justice demands more than polite words. Malevolent interdependence is a reality: to make benevolent interdependence an equally compelling reality demands a willingness by the powerful to recognize their own sovereignty cannot guarantee either their liberty or their security, and that unless they pool their sovereignty, weakening their own hold on it, its fruits will grow ever more tenuous. The idealism of Kant must await the realism of Hobbes if interdependence is to be tamed and malevolent globalization democratized.

This is not to suggest that the gradual construction of a post-sovereign global order must await the coming of a global Leviathan. Free societies were built bottom up as well as top down, and a social foundation of civic institutions and citizenship facilitates the emergence of sovereign government. This Tocquevillean lesson applies to global governance no less than national governance. Which is to say, citizens need not await presidents or governments to embrace interdependence and work to construct a civic architecture of global cooperation. For the challenge is how to get 'sovereign' political policy to catch up to global realities. While governments work to pool sovereignty and its police powers, citizens can work towards greater transnational civic cooperation.

Fashioning a global civil society that rests on global civic education and global citizenship will not ensure global governance, but it is an indispensable condition for global governance. Citizens, whether local or global, are made not born: educated and socialized into their roles rather than natural inhabitants of those roles. That was the lesson taught by the American founders when Thomas Jefferson and John Adams both recognized that without educated citizens the experimental new constitution would never work. In James Madison's words, a bill of rights and a constitution were not worth the parchment on which they were written in the absence of educated citizens who could make those documents work in practice.

The challenge today, then, is to create the foundations for global governance from below even as governments and international organizations face the challenge of giving teeth to their common covenants. The tools here will be technologies like the internet (already being used by malevolent NGOs such as al-Qaida and international right-wing movements like the neo-Nazis and the America militia movement) and cooperation among NGOs on the model of Civicus (the alliance of civil society organizations), the Community of Democracies, the Madrid Club (of ex-Presidents), the International Ethnic Collegium and Jubilee 2000 (aiming to erase third world debt). Their spirit has been expressed in the new Declaration of Interdependence, promulgated in 2003 and celebrated in a first 'Interdependence Day' festival in Philadelphia and Budapest in 2003 and again in 2004 in Rome and the September 11 memorial weekend (Interdependence Day is 12 September; see www.civworld.org for more). It is in the spirit both of these remarks and David Held's essay to end by citing this Declaration (see box overleaf).

DECLARATION OF INTERDEPENDENCE

We the people of the world do herewith declare our inter-dependence both as individuals and legal persons and as peoples – members of distinct communities and nations. We do pledge ourselves citizens of one CivWorld, civic, civil and civilized. Without prejudice to the goods and interests of our national and regional identities, we recognize our responsibil-ities to the common goods and liberties of humankind as a whole.

We do therefore pledge to work both directly and through the nations and communities of which we are also citizens:

> To establish democratic forms of global civil and legal gov-ernance through which our common rights can be secured and our common ends realized;

> To guarantee justice and equality for all by establishing on a firm basis the human rights of every person on the planet, ensuring that the least among us may enjoy the same liber-ties as the prominent and the powerful;

> To forge a safe and sustainable global environment for all – which is the condition of human survival – at a cost to peoples based on their current share in the world's wealth;

> To offer children, our common human future, special atten-tion and protection in distributing our common goods, above all those upon which health and education depend; and

> To foster democratic policies and institutions expressing and protecting our human commonality; and still at the same time,

> To nurture free spaces in which our distinctive religious, ethnic and cultural identities may flourish and our equally worthy lives may be lived in dignity, protected from polit-ical, economic and cultural hegemony of every kind.

Interdependence Day and the Declaration of Inter-dependence whose promulgation it marks allow new global citizens to move beyond both the horrors of 9/11 and the uncertainties of the war in Iraq and affirm the cre-ative potential of what is for now merely a grim reality. Without institutional enforcement, it is true, common civic work will not be enough. But without greater civic engagement in global governance, we are unlikely to secure anything resembling global enforcement. In a world where there are both doctors without frontiers and health plagues without frontiers, workers without frontiers and warming without frontiers, markets without frontiers and munitions without frontiers, surely it is time for citizens without frontiers. Not as a hope of wistful idealism but as a mandate of uncomfortable realism. The simple fact is that no American child will ever again sleep safe in her bed if children in Baghdad or Karachi or Nairobi are not secure in theirs. That Europeans will not be permitted to feel proud of liberty if people elsewhere feel humiliated by servitude. This is not because America is responsible for everything that has happened to others or because Europe was once the imperial colonizer of the world, but because in a world of interdependence the consequences of misery and injustice for some will be suffered by all. Because to be rich and powerful is not only to impact the whole earth, like it or not, but to reap the consequences, like it or not.

10

Globalization's Reality Check

John Elkington

The world's targets for sustainable development, codified in the Millennium Development Goals, can only be met by concerted action from governments, business and civil society. But if proposals for a 'global covenant' have meaning, it is time for companies to get real, says John Elkington.

A love of the sort of tennis played in the Wimbledon finals is good preparation for the knockabout entertainment of openDemocracy's contest between David Held and a star-studded cast of opponents and semi-sympathizers – from Martin Wolf, Meghnad Desai and Roger Scruton to Maria Livanos Cattaui and Grahame Thompson. At the same time, I can't be the only reader to feel increasingly frustrated as the rackets twang, balls sizzle by and competing line-calls are made.

The ultimate answers to the questions posed seem unlikely to plop neatly into the 'either/or' box favoured by the tidy-minded. Instead, they will ricochet across the 'both/and' space for decades before any moderately comprehensible – and moderately sustainable – outcome emerges.

Unlike some contributors, I sympathize with much of David Held's analysis. The old order is demonstrably unsustainable. We are at a turning point. The more gung-ho globalizers have lost some of their confidence in the historic inevitability of liberalization, privatization and, to a considerable degree, Americanization. There is growing concern that the world is failing to get a grip on a series of challenges in areas such as security, trade and environmental change, particularly climate change. And the United Nations system is radically dysfunctional.

As a long-time student of history, the older I get the more of a believer I become in catastrophism – that is that change comes in sudden bursts rather than gradually. Experience suggests that vested interests ensure that, while specialists and activists may argue until they're blue in the face about issues like security, ozone depletion or climate change, it's only when the system has to cope with an ozone hole, 9/11 or some other mega-shock that decision-makers (and ordinary citizens) 'get' the need for change.

Such shocks are guaranteed. In fact, creative destruction comes in many forms – economic, social, political, ecological – and the twenty-first century will see more of it than any previous one. Demographic trends, pandemics, financial crashes, disruptive technologies, the rise of some emerging economies into geopolitical positions unimaginable in today's world: all these will help create the political conditions in which new forms of global governance will evolve.

The millennium goals: ambition and reality

And there are a number of principles which will likely help shape emergent patterns of global governance. Let me briefly draw on work done earlier in 2004 by my colleagues and me at SustainAbility for the United Nations's global compact and five sponsoring companies (Daimler–Chrysler, Novartis, Novo Nordisk, Pfizer, SAP).

In contrast to Martin Wolf's neatly argued assertions in his chapter above, SustainAbility's report *Gearing Up: From Corporate Responsibility to Good Governance and Scalable Solutions* concludes that current initiatives designed to achieve the objectives outlined in the Millennium Development Goals have little chance of being successful on any meaningful timescale.

This assessment includes the UN global compact. While recent announcements suggest that the compact is trying to address questions over its credibility, there is a real risk that it will devolve to the convoy-adapted-to-the-speed-of-the-slowest-vessel mode operated by so many trade and industry federations, including Maria Livanos Cattaui's own International Chamber of Commerce.

There is, moreover, a real risk that the global compact will put the UN's wider reputation in jeopardy. All such voluntary initiatives are likely to be viewed with healthy scepticism, particularly where their 'business models' combine rapid recruitment with a lack of integrity measures for their corporate members or signatories.

SustainAbility's *Gearing Up* report addresses precisely the question of how to help ensure the integrity measures essential in the long term to organizations like the global compact. While scaling up the dialogue is obviously important, increasing the momentum of practical, on-the-ground responses on issues like climate change, HIV/Aids and corruption control is much more important. So, we argue, global compact members should be invited to report regularly on what they are specifically doing to address targets such as those set by the Millennium Development Goals.

We conclude that, despite achieving impressive progress in places, the international corporate responsibility (CR) movement is now bumping up against real limits. Most company initiatives are too peripheral from core businesses, too isolated from one another and too disconnected from wider systems to make much of a collective impact. Clearly, pessimism can be self-fulfilling, but the debate needs a challenge to the 'business-as-usual-will-solve-it' thinking which Martin Wolf's analysis might encourage in some readers.

In October 2003 the global compact asked us to evaluate the extent to which CR initiatives are helping drive the transition to more sustainable forms of development. In particular, we were asked to consider whether good corporate performance can act as a stimulus to bring about the governance improvements that will be necessary to make progress towards realizing the MDGs. In our case studies, we focused on climate change, corruption and health, in the form of HIV/Aids and chronic diseases.

Frankly, I'm worried. Despite high-level buy-in to both the priorities and targets of the MDGs, we found growing pessimism about the ability to achieve them within the agreed timescale. For example, the global governance initiative (GGI), hosted by the World Economic Forum (WEF), has concluded that – at best – collective global initiatives to achieve progress on goals like the MDGs are only 30–40 per cent effective.

Scorecards on our case study issues are equally worrying. Total CO_2 emissions worldwide have increased by 8.9 per cent since 1990, compared with the 60 per cent reduction the Intergovernmental Panel on Climate Change (IPCC) has called for by 2050. In the poorest countries, less than 10 per cent of the 6 million people who need antiretroviral medicines currently get them. Chronic diseases, such as diabetes, are rapidly emerging as a global pandemic. Corruption is proving an intractable challenge. In short, the combined actions of governments, business and civil society to address sustainable development issues are being outpaced by the problems.

Making 'responsibility' real

As ever, there is good news and bad. The good news is that many corporate responsibility initiatives are evolving in the right direction, with a growing variety of companies acknowledging a wider range of stakeholders and acting on an increasing number of key issues. The bad news is that most such initiatives still remain distanced from the company's core business activities, disengaged from long-term strategy. As a result, even leading companies pursue disjointed and at times conflicting activities, for example lobbying for lower social and environmental standards.

The CR movement has evolved in the context of weak, indeed often weakening, government leadership. It has made real progress, but is constrained by a lack of appropriate links to wider global, regional and national governance frameworks. Equally, few companies have so far sought to create CR-related market opportunities, to evolve relevant new business models or to encourage government policy development and action in line with their stated CR goals.

A small but growing number of bold and visionary companies have made considerable strides and are to be commended for their achievements. But their numbers will remain small as long as the business case for getting in front of the corporate pack remains weak. Here, government involvement will be crucial.

Some of the respondents to SustainAbility's survey noted, and it is a point we firmly endorse, that the critical task is not to get companies to adopt the responsibilities of governments but to help ensure governments fulfil their own responsibilities. Our case studies all underscore the crucial roles that governments must play: in setting the course, developing incentives and generally helping to create a stronger business case.

Here, I am fairly agnostic between Maria Livanos Cattaui and David Held on whether a 'global compact' or a 'global covenant' is the more needed. I agree with Cattaui that populism and simplistic solutions are dangerous, that there is no single, monolithic solution, and that – whatever we do – markets and business will be central. I also agree that initiatives like the global compact are networks for change rather than institutions for governance; but this does not alter the fact that a dangerous vacuum exists where global governance should be – and the United Nations, its agencies and its initiatives should be helping us all to focus our efforts in this area.

Yet I also share Held's conclusion that neoliberalism and unilateralism offer limited (or at least unattractive) long-term solutions to the global problems the world faces. The global compact is well placed to help both business and other partners to debate and shape the global operating system for twenty-first-century governance and markets. But to do so, and in a legitimate, effective way, it will need to address key reputational issues of its own.

The new focus on governance means that many such voluntary initiatives will need to meet higher levels of transparency and accountability. As they do, external stakeholders will be concerned to ensure that participants do not use voluntary initiatives merely as camouflage or alibis. My sense is that too many companies are currently using initiatives like the global compact as political cover, in the same way that small fish in the vast wastes of the ocean shoal under drifting rafts and other debris.

Both the United Nations as a whole and the global compact have the potential to be much more than that. But they are going to need energetic, consistent and sustained pressure to help them adapt to a new century and its challenges.

11

Three Modes of Ordering amidst Globalization

Takashi Inoguchi

Inoguchi emphasizes the major schisms in global politics which make a new global covenant unlikely even if it is desirable. He emphasizes the ad hoc and incremental qualities of change in the global order.

For years David Held has been a principal author of the argument for global democracy with a human face. His lucid and forceful style of writing solidly grounded on his version of social democracy writ large on a global scale makes him a favourite author on the subjects of democracy, global governance and globalization. David Held argues against:

1 indiscriminately applying to countries unbridled market mechanisms with market efficiency as their canon, which would only result in an intolerable gap between rich and poor and in producing a hotbed of dissenting voices from those oppressed below;
2 designing, engineering and imposing a kind of democracy that is both technocratic and elitist – and as defined in Washington DC – which would only result in a proliferation of regimes with feeble grass-roots and thus will not secure peace and sustainability in the third world.

In his opening chapter he has boldly set up the agenda of a social democratic covenant. In order to alleviate and redress some major malaises of globalization, neither the Washington Consensus on economic development in the third world nor the Washington security agenda would be of great assistance in attaining the safety, security and well-being of individuals in the third world because of their single-minded stress on military means. Instead, he proposes a social democratic global covenant with the following features:

1 Contractual arrangements should be allowed to frame globalization because market mechanisms are often insufficient to redress market externalities such as global warming and income inequalities.
2 Contractual arrangements should be allowed to alleviate some of the negative consequences of globalization such as failed states and anarchic societies.
3 Such contractual arrangements should be made in the spirit of formulating a global covenant, a set of quasi-binding guidelines of global action.
4 Such contractual arrangements should be financed largely through multilateral institutions, non-governmental organizations, national governments and business and individual donations.

I would agree with him if conditions were sufficiently ripe and ready for installing such a contractual regime at the global level. It seems that even if conditions are ripe and ready, as has been well and lucidly argued by David Held, modes of ordering the world differ substantially among key actors. I will use the remaining pages to make the point that the modi operandi and underlying structures make the task more difficult to attain.

Pascal Lamy on Japan, Europe and America in economic negotiations

In a newspaper interview in 2004, Pascal Lamy, then a key negotiator representing the European Union in trade and economic diplomacy, gave an illustrative characterization of economic diplomacy among the three major actors: Japan, Europe and America. America uses a megaphone to begin with, announcing the position it believes to be the final outcome of the negotiations at hand; Europe uses a telephone to start with, getting a feeling of and sounding out what adversaries have in mind; Japan keeps silent, trying to see what the other partners in the negotiation have to say on the subject and thereafter figuring out what position to take. Though simplistic, Pascal Lamy, an adroit player and astute observer who has been long on the scene, has captured the serious differences in their modi operandi. They are a reflection of their structural bases.

- A unipolar America merely announces. What it seeks is that its adversaries share its beliefs. Rallying round the flag is what it normally hopes for and often gets, even if very often this is little more than an ad hoc coalition of the temporarily willing.
- An enlarged Europe needs consultation among member states before, during and after the negotiations concerned. As befits the time-honoured continent of diplomacy, Europe engages with adversaries with tenacity and finesse. However, the larger it gets, the more divergent its own preferences become.
- As a polity which is essentially decentralized at the top level, Japan keeps having fights with itself – that is, among competing agencies pluralistically representing Japan at the negotiating table. Thus Japan confines itself to listening to the adversaries at the start, while during

the break the negotiators representing individual agencies (such as the ministries of economics and industry, of agriculture, forestry and fishing, of health, labour and welfare, and of foreign affairs, for instance, in one of the bilateral free trade negotiations) negotiate among themselves.

Madrid accord of 2003

The Madrid accord is meant to combine forces and resources to help a new Iraq to restore order and to recover and develop its economy through financial and technical assistance drawn from the United States, the World Bank, the United Nations, Japan and other industrialized countries. It represents just one instance of cooperating together to alleviate the negative consequences arising in the war-battered country called Iraq. The Iraq war may not, of course, be a good example of what we are seeking when we try to see how contractual arrangements can be of use in ameliorating situations after a third world country has been weakened by bankruptcy, defeat and/or regime change.

Needless to say, the Iraq war was in part the consequence of American unilateralism. Furthermore, the Iraq war created the great schism of the West, with the United States and the United Kingdom on the one side and France, Germany and Russia on the other side. The North Atlantic Treaty Organization did not work in Iraq as effectively as it did in Kosovo. The United Nations did not work in Iraq as effectively as it did in East Timor. Therefore it is no wonder that the Madrid accord has not had the vigorous participation of many actors. Apart from the World Bank and the United Nations, the United States and Japan are the only two major donors to the cause. Since much of the money that comes to Iraq through those international institutions originates in funds from Japan, the Japanese government feels strongly that Japan should be regarded as a substantial pillar of the Madrid accord.

The point here is that the way contractual accords like the Madrid accord, the Kyoto protocol and the Human Rights Declaration are shaped and accumulated is best described as ad hoc-ish and incremental.

Guiding principles for a global covenant

David Held's latest book, *Global Covenant*, reflects one of the structural conditions for a social democratically inspired global contractual agreement. In contrast, Anne-Marie Slaughter's book, *A New World Order*,[1] exemplifies the approach of pragmatically and incrementally shaped webs of agreements and practices made up of interactions, consultation, coordination and cooperation – treated as a global covenant, if global covenant is the appropriate word. It puts bureaucratic agencies, corporate departments and non-governmental organizations under the same umbrella called global governance, heavily overshadowed by the premise of the Pax Americana. In a further contrast to David Held, Robert Jackson's book, *The Global Covenant*,[2] represents the normatively oriented British tradition of the international society approach, with the Westphalian sovereign states retaining the legitimacy to assert themselves, yet with the diversity-accommodating club of countries being held together to get the earth going.

Although these three books are not meant to represent any particular ideologies or political tendencies, it is still interesting to see the broad differences guiding these authors as they portray global covenant and global governance in their respectively consistent and coherent fashions.

David Held's guiding spirit is social democratic, corresponding to when West European social democracies see some impasses. Anne-Marie Slaughter's is liberal democratic, corresponding to when the United States needs the global market, global finance and global institutions to run the affairs of global governance at times when it does not want to do so in a single-handed manner. Robert Jackson's is normatively concerned conservative, linked to when unipolar America focuses distortingly and dangerously on military power in Michael Mann's sense[3] and leaves most other concerns to the global market, the World Bank, the United Nations and the coalition of the willing.

Looked at from another angle, it may be argued that David Held, Anne-Marie Slaughter and Robert Jackson each represent one of the three necessary ingredients to get global governance functioning well and vigorously. They are respectively (1) a meeting of minds, (2) a sharing of beliefs, and (3) an overlap of interests. Needless to say, differing weights of these three ingredients are assigned by these three authors to the global covenant or global governance. That is all fine. But it is in everyone's interest to know how these ingredients can mingle and evolve to produce a newly synthesized global covenant and global governance. What we are seeing is that 'the sheer pre-eminence of American power [constitutes] the ordering and the taming principle of a disorderly and dangerous world'.[4]

12

The Debate on Globalization: Two New Contributions

Narcís Serra

The Washington Consensus and security doctrine have an Achilles' heel in common, argues Serra. They both suffer from a lack of legitimacy that needs to be urgently addressed by a robust democratic and multilateral politics.

With his outline of a new social democratic agenda for increasing world governability, David Held fostered a good debate on openDemocracy. I concur with him that the final objective of the debate should be to formulate proposals on how to govern globalization.

In his opening chapter, he indicates two issues blocking the way towards greater world governance: in the economic field of international relations, the so-called Washington Consensus; and in the area of international security, what he calls the Washington security agenda. These are not the only ones, nor does Held say that they are. The two issues are linked to the capital of the United States. This could seem opportunistic or inefficient, and some of this has been said in some of the commentaries in the debate on openDemocracy. Opportunistic, in centring the discussion on the US and on the attitude of its administration in a presidential election year, and also when the failure of the US policy in Iraq is clear.

Inefficient, because the elections have already taken place and George W. Bush has been ratified by the ballot boxes.

Personally, I think that they are two questions of the utmost significance in the effort to strengthen the governance of this progressively globalized world. The United States obviously cannot be declared the cause of the planet's ills, as David Mepham appropriately points out to us in his contribution to this debate, but it is clear that an attitude different from that of the leading world power could be a great impetus for governing globalization. Lately, I have been working on the two issues, collaborating with Mary Kaldor on the report on *A Human Security Doctrine for Europe* (see her account in appendix B below), and also organizing a seminar on 'From the Washington Consensus towards a new global governance' in Barcelona. The seminar brought together a large number of economists specializing in economic growth, most of them from the US, and, in addition to the articles they all contributed, produced a brief text subscribed to by the participants entitled 'The Barcelona Development Agenda' (see appendix A below). This, to me, seems like a good foundation to build on, as it has the agreement of a large and diverse group of leading economists. I recognize that it is very difficult – if not impossible – to be an expert on two such distinct issues, but one can work on the two if the objective is to foster discussion. I would like to add my voice to this debate with four reflections on legitimacy, the bottom-up approach, institutional reform and multilateralism. The four points are present in the two discussions I have mentioned, and they are also interlinked.

Legitimacy

Both the Washington Consensus and the Washington security agenda have an Achilles' heel in common which becomes more evident as time goes by. They suffer from a lack of legitimacy. Legitimacy is a concept which is not easy to spell out, but we could define it as the recognition on the part of public opinion that an action, albeit a politically debatable one, has been taken by the appropriate authority and that it is following accepted legal rules and procedures.

Reality has shown the US administration that the unilateral use of the enormous military might it possesses is not enough to convert this power into international order. To turn it into world order, legitimacy is necessary. Indeed, despite its power, in imposing its will unilaterally the United States disturbs international order instead of reinforcing it. That is, it increases world disorder. Recently, some extreme neocons, like Richard Perle, have written that something has been done wrong in the war in Iraq, since what was supposed to have been a liberation has become a military occupation. In the first place, it must be underscored that any military operation led by the classic military logic is doomed to political failure in a globalized world, and US military power is so great that it does not favour a rigorous renewal of its security and strategic doctrine, even if it has progressively incorporated the surprising capabilities afforded to it by the new technologies. But, above all, it must be taken into account that a large part of the difference that has existed between the proclaimed liberation and the occupation of Iraq is due to the operation's lack of international legitimacy.

Regaining international legitimacy on the part of the United States is a task which is not easy, and perhaps not probable either. For this, it would have to progress in three areas:

- A clear disposition to comply with international laws, agreements and procedures.
- An attitude of consultation, debate and agreement with other countries.

• A willingness to defend global interests, which, in the majority of cases, coincide with those of the United States.

As I have said, it is not probable that these changes in direction will occur in George W. Bush's second term. This leads us to analyse whether there are possibilities of advancing in the direction proposed by David Held, given the current attitude of the US administration. In his contribution to this discussion, Roger Scruton states that for this reason a global pact based on a social democratic consensus is not possible. But, in support of David Held's optimism, we can put forward the idea that the need for international legitimacy is so clear (even Robert Kagan defends this with convincing arguments) that we can expect some changes in this direction. The seeking of legitimacy is a foundation on which many of the political actions that David Held includes in his social democratic consensus can be built.

Bottom-up approach

A common path for advancing in the direction proposed by David Held, both in relation to the Washington Consensus and to security policy, could be called the 'bottom-up approach'. This, in the report *A Human Security Doctrine for Europe*, is explicitly included as one of the main proposals for a new European security doctrine, not only as a moral question but also as a necessary element of effectiveness.

In the case of the declaration of the economists gathered in Barcelona, this approach is reflected in the statement that necessary institutional reforms are specific to each country and that 'encouraging developing nations to copy mechanically the institutions of rich countries – as the international financial institutions tend to do – is not guaranteed to yield results, and can do more harm than good'. But, above all, it is seen when they point out that 'there is no single set of policies that can be guaranteed to ignite sustained growth' and that the developing countries should have the freedom to experiment with the policies they consider appropriate to their specific circumstances. In fact, possibly the most serious defect of the Washington Consensus (understood, as Held does, as referring to the practices of US administrations and some international financial institutions) has been to believe that there exists a single model for promoting development which could – and should – be applied in a general way, that is, from above. David Held, citing Dani Rodrik, defends this position, and I believe that it is significant that it is subscribed to by economists from a wide range of viewpoints, like those gathered in Barcelona. (Maria Livanos Cattaui also adopts this position when she defends the idea that we do not need just a single alternative to the Washington Consensus.)

Institutions

Both the security report and the development agenda are fully in keeping with the recent trend, accepted even by the international financial institutions, to consider that institutions matter. In regard to the human security doctrine for Europe (HSDE), the report makes a great effort both to demonstrate the need for and to provide guidelines for a new legal framework that would govern a decision to intervene and the operations of intervention themselves.

The Barcelona Development Agenda defends the idea that an appropriate balance between the market and the state is at the heart of successful development strategies. It is a great advance with respect to the neoliberal position, according to which it is believed that the smaller the state, the better. It is also a great advance with respect to so many economists who have believed that it is enough to concentrate on the economy to diagnose and give impetus to economic growth. In the case of the economists, a greater humility continues to be advisable: these institutional reforms, like those in the sphere of elections, justice or anti-corruption, are called second generation; for them, those of the first generation continue to be privatizations, the liberalization of the capital market or flexible exchange rates.

Multilateralism

Although it does not use the word frequently, David Held's contribution signifies a strong defence of multilateralism as a way of governing globalization. This issue is repeatedly dealt with by almost all of the participants in the debate. Maria Livanos Cattaui states, 'I am a huge believer in multilateral approaches to such challenges' (as might be constituted by the world's agrarian problems). Meghnad Desai accepts that a new world order will come, but not from a new agreement, which he considers to be top-down and statist, but rather because it is demanded by movements of population and capital, and by the multinational companies. When Roger Scruton expresses support for the 'old covenant, enshrined in treaties between nation-states', he is manifesting his lack of confidence in multilateral solutions.

Martin Wolf is the one who most directly opposes the strengthening of multilateralism. He considers that the ambitious reconstruction of institutions is unnecessary, because the rich countries can reduce their agricultural protectionism or increase their development aid without the need for multilateral institutions. With regard to security, he is even more radical: 'designing a new multilateral security system is a largely idle exercise' while US military power is maintained.

This position adopted by Martin Wolf is not totally coherent with the one he himself maintains in his recent book *Why Globalization Works*. Of the ten commandments with which he concludes it, he devotes two to supranational institutions which are to produce global public goods, which, to his mind, should be 'specific, focused and enforceable'. The theory of rational decision tells us that if personal interest is pursued in relation to the production of a public good, the equilibrium result is that nobody contributes and for this reason there is a non-existence of this good (the prisoner's dilemma outcome). The same occurs on an international scale, and multilateralism has to go with a set of laws and procedures that move countries to contribute jointly to the production of the global public good.

I agree with David Held when he says that 'over the coming few years between now and 2010, choices will be made that will determine the fate of the globe for decades to come'. It is necessary to create a system of global governance that is more efficient and easier for all countries, before China, India, and also Brazil, become first-order world powers. It may be too late to think about multilateralism as a path to a solution in a few years.

The defence of multilateralism is another of the common traits in the two documents that I have been commenting on. The report on human security considers multilateralism to be one of the essential principles of the new doctrine for European security, and it defines it as closely related to the concept of legitimacy. The Barcelona Agenda proposes advancing through multilateral negotiations on international trade and recommends the reformation of institutions and international economic agreements so that the developing countries participate with adequate representation in these organisms.

In conclusion, David Held has not only opened up an important debate in a provocative way, but he has also done so at a most opportune time, as can be seen by the fact that his essay has given rise to many seminars and conferences on the two issues he brings up, among them the ones I have been citing here.

I do not want to end these comments without an epilogue on Europe's role in the objective of governing globalization. Europe is the most highly evolved political actor among those which have resulted from multilateralism. It must promote the adoption of this kind of solution in the two areas contemplated by David Held. In that of security, the human security proposal of the HSDE is one development which is coherent with the security strategy elaborated by Javier Solana's team and approved by the European Council in December 2003. In this sense, we must demand a more determined, more responsible attitude on the part of the EU as a 'norms promoter', as called for by the HSDE report, and greater advances towards the goal of the effective multilateralism that has marked the EU itself. The basic problem in this direction is not a lack of military capabilities but rather of political will. One way to spur it on is to promote debate in the heart of civil society. This is what David Held has been doing, and also what has been carried out by the experts who have drawn up the report on a human security doctrine for Europe and the Barcelona Development Agenda.

13

A Covenant to Make Global Governance Work

Anne-Marie Slaughter and Thomas N. Hale

Cosmopolitanism and nationalism cannot be treated as mutually exclusive. In a sharp and constructive critique of Held's position, Slaughter and Hale argue for a new conception of moral responsibilities and institutional politics that transcends this old dichotomy.

With his usual talent for broad thinking and synthesis, David Held has sketched a compelling vision of a cosmopolitan global order. While not moving significantly beyond his previous work – and that of other scholars like John Ruggie – Held's essay and his book *Global Covenant* forcefully present the contemporary challenges of global governance. More importantly, they outline the kind of law-based, just and equitable global order needed to resolve these challenges democratically – a 'global covenant' that institutes the principles of social democracy across the globe.

Unlike some other contributors, we do not dispute the desirability of Held's vision. If others have found bogeymen lurking in the essay, we suspect it is largely because the level of abstraction at which Held is writing allows them to read their own fears into his work.

Nonetheless, for those concerned with actual policy, abstraction is itself problematic. Held does offer a number of specific policy recommendations in the essay, all of which he develops further in *Global Covenant*. However, the more concrete and politically feasible of his recommendations seem insufficient to institute his far-reaching vision, while the larger proposals tend to be underspecified or politically unrealistic.

This lack of workable policy options is not a flaw of Held's essay per se, but rather, as Maria Livanos Cattaui has pointed out, a shortcoming of global governance scholarship in general. The field, led by thinkers like Held, has made enormous progress towards conceptualizing the challenges of contemporary globalization. Unfortunately, it has devoted fewer efforts towards designing specific, innovative and realistic governance techniques that use these conceptual advances to improve people's lives.

This abundance of vision and shortage of action plans is not limited to academia. In 2000 the G20, a network of finance ministers representing both developed and developing countries, endorsed the 'Montreal Consensus' as an alternative to the neoliberal Washington Consensus. The Montreal Consensus affirmed economic globalization as a powerful engine of growth, while also recognizing the need to complement liberalization with social programmes. At the millennium summit that same year all the members of the United Nations committed themselves to a series of Millennium Development Goals: setting concrete targets for efforts to combat poverty, disease, hunger and other ills. A year later the International Commission on Intervention and State Sovereignty, charged by UN Secretary-General Kofi Annan with rethinking humanitarian intervention in the wake of both the Rwanda and Kosovo crises, issued its report *The Responsibility to Protect*, charging all UN members with a duty to protect their own citizens and empowering the UN as a whole to intervene, under carefully specified conditions, if a member state committed grave and systematic human rights abuses against its own citizens.

The above examples suggest that significant agreement already exists in some of the areas Held advances, but also highlight how distant such ideas remain from implementation. Conceptualization, consensus, covenants, goals and principles are important first steps, but the challenge before cosmopolitan thinkers and policy-makers now is to find the policies and techniques that will make these visions real enough to actually help solve global problems.

Such policies must be innovative. Even if we could replicate domestic institutions at the international level, they would likely prove inadequate for the complexities of global governance.

Such policies must also be politically realistic. While cosmopolitans often emphasize what *could* be, their commitment to the world's very real and very current problems compels them to also consider what *can* be.

But how to be innovative and realistic about proposals to strengthen social justice in the world following an American election that has produced a government that rejects social democracy at home, much less abroad? Held explicitly defines his global covenant not only in contraposition to the Washington Consensus but also to the 'Washington security agenda' (pre-emptive war and hard-headed unilateralism). He clearly does not expect much comfort from the Bush administration.

But a Bush administration we have, and will have for four more years. And fulminating against Washington, both for Europeans and for American liberals, is not going to help. The US is a cause of some of the problems Held identifies, and it need not be part of the solution. It is certainly possible for Europe itself, or Europe in coalition with other countries around the world, to move some way towards achieving Held's vision without the US. But Held would certainly admit that the people in the world whom he seeks most to help – the hungry, the sick, the illiterate – will benefit far more from a pragmatic transatlantic effort than from four more years of fruitless sniping.

More generally, if we continue to define the challenges of global governance as a struggle between progressive, cosmopolitan forces and conservative, nationalist ones, then cosmopolitanism will lose. This is a key conceptual point with a number of very practical implications. And it is a point that must be made and heard in terms of substance as well as style.

Much of the post-election soul-searching among Democrats in the US has focused on the need to put aside feelings of intellectual superiority and moral disdain for the Bush administration and its base. The self-satisfaction such sentiments provide is not worth the political damage they can cause. The same message needs to be heard and heeded by progressives across the Atlantic and indeed around the world.

At the level of style, one helpful response would be the professionalization of interstate relations, particularly the transatlantic relationship. Too many European politicians have scored political points at home through Bush-bashing, and the American President and his party have too frequently pandered to American anti-Europeanism. This rhetoric diminishes the ability of European countries and the US to work together and thus does a disservice to the European and American publics, not to mention the many other countries that benefit from transatlantic coordination. Both sides should abandon theatrics and focus on identifying the areas of agreement that can move policy forward.

At the much more fundamental level of substance, cosmopolitans like David Held should recognize nationalism as a serious force in the US and elsewhere and accept that it is unlikely to dissipate in the near future. George W. Bush was re-elected in part because the American public thought he was more patriotic than his opponent. Though large swaths of Europe seem increasingly post-national – as do many members of the elite and the intelligentsia in the US and around the world – the vast majority of the world continues to attach great importance to national identities. Even in Europe, the genius of the EU has been precisely to foster greater integration without destroying the distinct national identities and cultures of European states, identities now expressed on the football field rather than the fields of battle.

Instead of presenting cosmopolitanism and nationalism as an age-old dichotomy, one that all too often equates in the public mind with left and right, cosmopolitans must seek instead to *harness* nationalism in the service of cosmopolitan ideals – ideals that are themselves often embedded in national creeds. Bush's rallying cry before vast audiences during the American election was 'Freedom is on the march'. His listeners, particularly among evangelical Christians, did not hear this as a cover for the cynical expansion of American empire, as many European critics would have it, but rather as a sincere effort to extend freedom to Iraqis as their human birthright. They may be misguided, even tragically deluded. But their vision fuses national and cosmopolitan ideals.

A very concrete way of dissolving the cosmopolitan/ nationalist divide would be to promote transgovernmental networks, global governance mechanisms composed of national government officials who perform similar functions in a variety of states. These networks are increasingly important in areas like financial regulation, environmental protection, jurisprudence and counterterrorism. While global in reach, transgovernmental networks are fundamentally connected to national governments and thus elide some of the legitimacy concerns and functional limitations that often face international organizations. At the same time, they should not be seen as an alternative to these more traditional organizations, but as a complement to them.

To take a topical example, Canada's Prime Minister is pushing to create a G20 at the leaders' level (L20). The current G20 of finance ministers includes Argentina, Australia, Brazil, Canada, China, France, Germany, India, Indonesia, Italy, Japan, Mexico, Russia, Saudi Arabia, South Africa, Korea, Turkey, the United Kingdom, the United States and the European Union, as well as representatives of the World Bank and the IMF. Paul Martin's version of the L20 would bring together the presidents and prime ministers of these countries, possibly including a few other countries depending on the issue at hand as well as a senior representative from the UN.

The Chinese and the French have been favourable towards this idea; it is likely that an initial meeting could happen in the fall of 2005. Because it is more representative of the world's people, the group is far more likely to advance the goals embedded in Held's global covenant than the G8 or the current UN Security Council. If the Security Council were to be suitably reformed, the need for the L20 might disappear; alternatively, it could continue to serve a vital link between the UN and the Bretton Woods institutions. In any event, it is an institutional structure serving a cosmopolitan agenda that nevertheless recognizes and embraces the power and perspectives of different nation-states.

Finally, cosmopolitans must equally deconstruct what often seems to be an implicit dichotomy between cosmopolitanism and religion. Here the United States provides an interesting laboratory for the world. Can the David

Helds of the world find a way to talk about their goals in a way that relates to the almost 60 million people who voted for George W. Bush? We suspect that there are actually a surprising number of issues on which David Held and the average Bush voter can agree. The problem is that they talk past each other.

Thus the first problem is once again stylistic – to find a language that connects cosmopolitan goals to Christian values. The shift also requires cosmopolitans to invoke Americans' longstanding belief in the basic institutions of self-government and liberty, the secular creed that many Americans hold just as dear as their religious beliefs. As Anatol Lieven has written on openDemocracy, Americans' faith in God and their faith in the institutions of democracy often intertwine, a mix cosmopolitans must take into account. Moreover, from Martin Luther to Martin Luther King Jr, religious values are often cosmopolitan values. Similarly, cosmopolitanism can be seen as a kind of global evangelism, a universal call to a better world.

We suggest a set of 'moral responsibilities' that are likely to resonate with Bush voters and encourage progress on global issues. Both Christian morality and civic virtue enjoin citizens, especially the powerful, to uphold the rights and freedoms of others. They impose a duty to help the poor, the sick and the disadvantaged, and they insist on responsible stewardship of God's creation. They require good people to have a decent respect and tolerance for the opinions of others. They teach that pride – jingoism included – is a sin, and that humility is a virtue. It was not without reason that during his first presidential campaign George W. Bush wooed his conservative base by speaking of a 'humbler' American foreign policy.

Lest our prescriptions be read as an effort to frame a global cosmopolitan debate only in terms of American politics and demographics, it is worth remembering the point made on openDemocracy by Dave Belden, president of the Unitarian Universalist Congregation of the Catskills, about the increasing numbers of evangelicals in the developing world. As American gays learned to their sorrow last year following the installation of a gay Episcopal bishop, the leading opponents of such a step were Anglican bishops and their congregations from Africa. It seems that what plays in the American south may play just as well in the global south.

These shifts in attitude and language, coupled with governance techniques that incorporate nation-states, may help to close the gap between the 'Washington world' and Held's vision of cosmopolitan social democracy. Many important issues are unlikely to yield consensus – causes such as the International Criminal Court, efforts to fund global governance projects through international taxation, and global environmental treaties. But for other issues of concern to cosmopolitans – the Aids pandemic, responsible humanitarian intervention, alleviation of global poverty – progress seems at least within the realm of possibility.

14

Three Crises and the Need for American Leadership

Kofi Annan

The United Nations is exploring how best to work with the United States and the international community to meet future global security threats. The UN Secretary-General, Kofi Annan, outlines the thinking behind the high-level panel he appointed to investigate this key twenty-first-century challenge.[1]

The United Nations matters: it offers the best hope of a stable world and a broadly equitable global order, based on generally accepted rules.

This assertion has been greatly questioned over the past year. But recent events have reaffirmed, and even strengthened, its validity. A rule-based system is in the interest of all countries – especially today. Globalization has shrunk the world. The very openness that is such an important feature of today's most successful societies also makes deadly weapons relatively easy to obtain, and terrorists relatively difficult to restrain. Today, the strong feel almost as vulnerable to the weak as the weak feel vulnerable to the strong.

It is in the interest of every country, therefore, to have international rules – and to observe them in practice. But such a system can only work if, in devising and applying the rules, the legitimate interests of all countries are accommodated, and decisions are reached collectively.

That is the essence of multilateralism: the founding principle of the United Nations. All great American leaders have understood this. That is one of the things that make the United States a unique world power. America feels the need to frame its policies, and exercise its leadership, not just in the light of its own particular interests, but also with an eye to international interests and universal principles.

Among the finest examples of this was the plan for reconstructing Europe after the Second World War which General George Marshall announced at Harvard in 1947. That was one part of a larger-scale and truly statesmanlike effort, in which Americans joined with others to build a new international system – one that largely worked, and survives in its essentials nearly sixty years later.

During these sixty years, the United States and its partners oversaw historic achievements: developing the United Nations; building an open world economy; promoting human rights and decolonization; and supporting the transformation of Europe into a democratic, cooperative community of states, such that war between them has become unthinkable.

The United States played a vital role in all these processes. It is, inextricably and indispensably, a part of the successful international system based on the primacy of the rule of law that America itself helped foster.

American power was and is an essential ingredient in the international order. But what makes that power effective, as an instrument of progressive change, is the legitimacy it gains from being deployed within a framework of international law and multilateral institutions, and in pursuit of the common interest. This has been demonstrated once again in recent times, in the way that the United States found that it needed the unique legitimacy of the United

Nations to bring into being a credible interim government in Iraq.

American leaders have generally recognized that other states, big and small, prefer to cooperate on the great issues of peace and security through multilateral institutions such as the United Nations, thus giving such cooperation legitimacy.

These leaders have accepted that others with a different view on a specific issue may on occasion be right. They have understood that true leadership is ultimately based on common values and a shared view of the future. Over six decades, whenever this approach has been applied consistently, it has proved a winning formula.

But today this rule-based international system is threatened by a triple crisis – one that challenges both the United Nations as a system and the United States as a global leader.

A triple crisis

This crisis is, first, one of collective security; second, one of global solidarity; and third, one of cultural division and distrust.

Security

To people in the global north, the security crisis often looks the most visible and therefore dangerous. The fear of international terrorism and of the spread of weapons of mass destruction – and of their combination – raises severe worry that existing rules governing the use of force might not supply adequate protection to citizens of many states.

This crisis came to a head in 2003 in the argument over Iraq. On one side, it was argued that force should be used only in the most compelling circumstances of self-defence – when you are already being attacked or clearly just about to be – or otherwise by a decision of the Security Council.

On the other side it was argued, in essence, that in the post-9/11 world preventive use of force has become necessary in some cases, because you can't afford to wait till you are sure that someone has weapons of mass destruction and is going to attack you: by then it may be too late.

Indeed, the combination of global terrorism, possible proliferation of weapons of mass destruction and the existence of rogue or dysfunctional states does face us with a new challenge. The United Nations was never meant to be a suicide pact. But what kind of world would it be, and who would want to live in it, if every country was allowed to use force, without collective agreement, simply because it thought there might be a threat?

I believe the way forward is clear, though far from easy. We cannot abandon our system of rules, but we do need to adapt it to new realities, and find answers to some difficult questions. When is use of force by the international community, acting collectively to deal with these new threats, justified? Who decides? And how should the decision be taken in time for it to be effective?

In November 2003 I appointed a panel of eminent persons to examine these questions, and suggest ways of making our United Nations work better, in an age when humanity needs the organization more than ever.

I expect their recommendations by the end of 2004,[2] and I hope that they will lead to wise decisions by governments. But panels and governments cannot change the world by themselves. They need not just good ideas but also sustained pressure from internationalists in all countries – people who are both visionary and pragmatic.

The issues go beyond terrorism and weapons of mass destruction. We also need better criteria for identifying, and clearer rules for dealing with, genocide and crimes against humanity. The problem here is that the international community often reacts too late and too weakly.

As Under-Secretary-General for Peacekeeping ten years ago I lived through the traumatic experiences of Bosnia and Rwanda, where UN peacekeeping forces had to witness appalling massacres but could do almost nothing to stop them, because there was no collective will to act.

And as Secretary-General I have warned that the Security Council cannot expect to be taken seriously unless it fulfils its responsibility to protect the innocent. National sovereignty was never meant to be a shield behind which massacres are carried out with impunity.

As things stand today, we still face too many cases where governments tolerate, incite, or even themselves perpetrate massacres and other crimes against international humanitarian law. In the Darfur region in western Sudan, for example, thousands of villages have been burnt and more than a million people forced from their homes. In all, about 1.3 million people need immediate assistance.

The international community must insist that the Sudanese authorities immediately put their own house in order. They must neutralize and disarm the brutal Janjaweed militia; allow humanitarian supplies and equipment to reach the population without further delays; ensure that the displaced people can return home in safety; and pursue the political negotiations on Darfur with a renewed sense of urgency. Further delay could cost hundreds of thousands of lives.

Solidarity

The second crisis is one of solidarity.

The different views among the world community about the war in Iraq should never have diverted its attention and resources away from the goals for reducing extreme poverty articulated in 2000 at the UN's millennium summit.

These Millennium Development Goals, whose target date for completion is 2015, include halving the proportion of people in the world without clean water to drink; making sure all girls, as well as boys, receive at least primary education; slashing infant and maternal mortality; and stopping the spread of HIV/Aids.

Governments and peoples in the poor countries themselves are responsible for achieving parts of this agenda. But richer countries, too, have a vital part to play. They must meet agreed targets on aid, trade and debt relief. American leadership is essential here too; and this is an issue that I'd like to hear Americans ask their presidential candidates about.

Unless we make the millennium goals a priority now, we shall soon run out of time to achieve them by 2015 – which means that millions of people will die, prematurely and unnecessarily, because we failed to act in time.

And we know, from bitter experience in Afghanistan and elsewhere, that our world will not be secure while citizens of entire countries are trapped in oppression and misery.

Division

The third crisis can be described as one of division, but more broadly as one of prejudice and intolerance. It is rooted in attitudes of fear or anger which lead to the treatment of those whose faith or culture differs from one's own as enemies.

We must not allow, for example, 'Islam' to be blamed or all Muslims to be suspected, because a small number of Muslims commit acts of violence and terror. Neither must we allow anti-Semitism to disguise itself as a reaction to Israeli government policies – any more than we should allow questioning of these policies to be silenced by accusations of anti-Semitism. And we must not allow Christians in the Muslim world to be treated as if their religion somehow made them a secret vanguard of Western imperialism.

It is in times of fear and anger, even more than in times of peace and tranquillity, that universal human rights, and a spirit of mutual respect, are most needed. This, in short, is a time when we must adhere to our global rulebook: a time when we must respect each other – as individuals, yes; but individuals who each have the right to define their own identity, and belong to the faith or culture of their choice.

These, then, are the three great tests that our system faces, in the first years of the new century. They might be described as:

- the test of collective security;
- the test of solidarity between rich and poor;
- the test of mutual respect between faiths and cultures.

These are tests – for the United Nations, the United States, and the entire international community of which we are part. We can pass them, but only if we live up to our best ideals and our best traditions.

15

What are the Dangers and the Answers? Clashes over Globalization

David Held

David Held's argument that the challenge of globalization requires a new 'global covenant' informed by social democratic political values provoked lively debate and strong disagreement. Here, he responds to his critics, clarifies his vision, and looks ahead.

Thank you openDemocracy and all those who have taken part in the debate on my essay 'Globalization: the dangers and the answers'. I have learnt a lot. Given how serious and demanding the issues are, it is important to remain open to learning from other voices – and it would be hard to imagine that anyone is entirely right about them all.

I am grateful in particular to Maria Livanos Cattaui, John Elkington, Takashi Inoguchi, David Mepham, Roger Scruton, Narcís Serra, Anne-Marie Slaughter and Thomas Hale, and Grahame Thompson, for their constructive engagement, and to Kofi Annan for the essential reminder he provides of the gravity of the issues facing us.

But the polemical stances of some contributors – notably Martin Wolf, Meghnad Desai and Jagdish Bhagwati[1] – make me uneasy. In the search for what they take to be enemies of economic globalization, they too often misconstrue, mischaracterize and mislead. Worse, I fear that they wilfully refuse to take on board the fact that those of us who are critics of the present form and character of economic globalization do so from a positive point of view. We recognize the material advances the global economy has achieved, but cannot accept the high costs to many communities and the environment. I strongly support international trade, but argue that it needs good, strong government to achieve its full potential. Bhagwati, Desai and Wolf misrepresent my argument and too often project it as a form of opposition to globalization in general.

The most important argument today, in my view, is over how globalization can and should be governed. This is the debate that really matters. My reply will be centred here, engaging with the lively responses to my essay and then refuting in closer detail the misrepresentations mentioned above.

The anti-globalizers: Patrick Bond

But first I will respond to Patrick Bond who does indeed reject globalization as we know it. Bond argues that my critique is not tough or deep enough. I respect the fact that he takes a different view of the form and limits of contemporary capitalism. His response to me is a clear and concise overview of the thinking behind the global justice movement. It deserves a fuller countercritique than I will present here. But to make the fundamental differences between us as clear as possible in a short space, it seems there are four key issues over which we disagree profoundly.

First, Bond believes that political reforms will always make things worse. He calls them 'reformist reforms'. By this he means politics as we know it. His is an argument that grossly underestimates the hugely significant welfare, democratic and human rights agendas that have made positive differences to millions of lives. Moreover, the counterfactual – that sweeping the existing system away with genuinely 'non-reformist reforms' would make for a radically better basis for human development – is entirely unproven. The history of Soviet communism starkly warns against such ambitions.

Second, he thinks that 'bottom up' is always better and wiser. But this is surely not the case. Social movements are by no means necessarily noble or wise. They are (naturally) riddled with disagreements and conflicting views. They may generate many important ideas and pressures, and his list of ideas that have emerged recently from the South African social justice movement is impressive. Against this, it needs to be borne in mind that opposing social groups exist on almost every issue and that is why the institutions and mechanisms of a responsive democracy matter.

Third, he clearly takes the view that all politics is essentially an expression of economic interests. Hence his disparaging remarks about how I characterize the post-Holocaust international reforms. His view here is typical of the deep Marxist misunderstanding of politics. Many currents of Marxism have tried to explain the political solely by reference to the economic and so have missed what they must learn from liberalism and other political traditions: that politics exists in its own distinct realm and that a pre-occupation with the nature and limits of politics is a question independent of economic matters. True, liberalism massively underestimates the significance of economic power. But critics of liberalism should not countenance the reverse error.

Fourth, Bond believes that the current crisis of globalization is really a crisis of world capitalism. I am unconvinced of this for many reasons. Among these are the diversity of forms of capitalism that exist in different regions of the world, the extraordinary durability of capitalism in its various guises (always underestimated by critics), and the clear absence of alternative political economies. Where we agree is that the 'neoliberal project' has often had pernicious effects and the move to replace it is of the utmost urgency for the life chances and life expectancy of the many.

These four positions typify a certain left attitude which bases its appeal on a humanism of the exploited but rests its logic on an unacceptable economic determinism. The two come together because the economic system of global capitalism is projected as one of systemic overproduction and superexploitation whose crisis will open the way for those untainted by their allegiance to the false consciousness of 'reformist reforms'.

However, for all the appalling and well-recorded consequences of contemporary globalization, it is a dynamic system that helps engender development and growth. That the United States may be heading for a crisis thanks to its trade and fiscal deficits and the recklessness of the Bush administrations does not mean that capitalism is on its last legs. On the contrary, the all too likely brutal 'correction' which many expect will be a sign of its continuing vitality and durability.

A revolution, driven solely by bottom-up politics and aiming to sweep aside liberal democracy and a supposedly fatally weakened global capitalism, is a wholly implausible objective. This leads us back to the debate about how most effectively to transform globalization today.

Global governance from below: Benjamin Barber

I am puzzled by Benjamin Barber's response to my opening chapter in the debate. He says that I rely 'on normative solutions that are as ethically unimpeachable as they are practically unrealizable'. By contrast, he roots himself in 'the realities of interdependence'. But surely, as he must know, most of my work over the last ten years has involved an analysis of interdependence. In works like *Global Trans-formations*[2] I and my co-authors have specifically examined the growing enmeshment of countries in dense networks of interconnectedness of the kinds he alludes to. Moreover, my chapter bases its normative reflections on an analysis of the failures of leading policies; the normative concerns emerge from a consideration of the dilemmas and prob-lems of the Washington Consensus and the Washington security agenda. Of course, in making recommendations to go beyond these policy packages, value judgements are involved, as they are in his own prescriptive preferences. My value preferences are clearly stated and linked to some well-established social movements and political traditions. They do not come from nowhere!

Barber emphasizes the importance of thinking about the way current global problems and challenges can no longer be resolved by the old political languages rooted exclusively in sovereign independence, national society and a world of sovereign nations. He notes how 'political philosophies rooted in independence' now face 'realities rooted in inter-dependence'. His intervention calls for new global institu-tions founded not merely on greater cooperation, but also on the means to enforce the mandates yielded by coopera-tion. In short, he champions the need for global govern-ance backed by a new 'global sword'. Yet he stresses that progress towards the construction of a post-sovereign global order does not need to await the creation of a global Leviathan. Instead, the creation of global social networks of civil society point the way forward. Global governance can be created from below. The tools here are new tech-nologies like the internet and cooperation among NGOs on the model of Civicus (the umbrella organization for NGOs and a number of leading social movements and organizations).

Barber's position is a familiar account of the importance of building social institutions from below and on the basis of the energies and creative skills of civil society. But while there is much to agree with here, the analysis reproduces many of the same failings as Patrick Bond's. A simple appeal to social movements and civil society cuts short critical reflection on how we can recognize progressive and regressive moments in these tendencies. Unless we have an independent critical framework, we have no means of recognizing whether social and political agents act with 'wisdom and nobility'. As in Bond, the analysis surrenders to an appeal to a seemingly self-evident progressive position. Sound political analysis has always depended on clear and rigorous accounts of what is ideal and desirable, robust empirical analyses of the circumstances of the time, and reflections on how to move from where we are to where we might like to go. Barber's appeal to civil society cuts short this enquiry.

The real argument: Maria Livanos Cattaui

Maria Livanos Cattaui thinks my overall proposals are 'pie in the sky'. She is a tireless participant in international negotiations. I respect her greatly for this. But I am not convinced by her claim that she champions practical and realistic ways forward, with sovereignty recognized as the single basis of politics. If only the matter were so straightforward.

Increasingly, our world is one of overlapping communities of fate, not of the national determination of destiny. Whether one is concerned with trade, finance, drugs, security or the environment, one is inescapably concerned with a range of processes and forces which cut across borders and require global public goods for their open and effective regulation. This interconnected world is, of course, heavily shaped by the huge imbalances of power relations found in the interstate system. The decisions of the most powerful countries about many matters that appear domestic can ramify across borders and make others into passive recipients of the effects of these decisions. If we add to this the way in which the global economy, global communications and global politics generate processes and forces which wash across borders, it is easy to see that it is Maria Livanos Cattaui who is the idealist – an idealist for the lost world of discrete national states and their discrete national fortunes.

We live with, and we need, multilayered, multilevel governance for different kinds of political challenges at different levels, local, national, regional and global. The question is: will such governance arrangements be accountable and democratic, or will they be a reflection of the existing asymmetries of power which privilege some political and economic actors?

Cattaui asks, who would govern a global covenant? I find this an odd question. You could ask who would govern a human rights regime and conclude that because there was no single relevant agency there should not be a human rights regime. A new global covenant, like the covenant that emerged at the international level after the Holocaust, would offer a new framework of understanding, agreement and rules for governments, civil society and business.

There is no single answer to who would govern such an understanding, for it would of course be a diversity of actors, agencies and institutions at different levels. But unlike the current motley set of interstate organizations and agencies, the functions and operations of these actors and collectivities would be bound by the requirements of democracy and social justice.

Cattaui strongly disagrees with monolithic answers; so do I. Hence I take issue with the policy packages of the Washington Consensus and the Washington security doctrine. As I have said, a global covenant would comprise many different agencies and policy initiatives operating in many different domains within and across borders. This is not a monolith: it is about diverse bodies and organizations working within rule systems which entrench social, welfare, environmental and human rights concerns. The difference from the status quo is that these concerns would be central to the processes of globalization – not marginal as at present.

The political problems we face today also include the fragmentation of jurisdictions. In the current global order there are distinctive sets of rules and domains of law which diverge from each other and often do not inform each other. If the rules concerning economics, human rights and the environment do not mesh with each other they risk simply referring to distinct and separate spheres, with the likely result of generating massive unregulated externalities affecting health and the global commons, among other areas.

Cattaui is in favour of networks of change, like those initiated by the global compact. These are important indeed. But as John Elkington reports, they can be weak, with little enforcement capacity. The essential rationale of political authority is to uphold the rule of law and impartial application of rules. Thus, I argue, in the world of multilevel problems we need effective multilevel political powers. Terrorism, global warming, HIV/Aids will not be resolved by loose networks of change. These networks need enforcement capacities and need to be accountable to public governance structures if democracy, not sectional interests, is to prevail.

To put it simply, in response to Cattaui: there needs to be effective and accountable global governance, but this does not mean that there has to be a single 'government' of globalization.

America and globalization: Roger Scruton

Roger Scruton also attacks my call for global forms of political authority. I agree with aspects of his anti-statist arguments, both as they relate to communism and as they relate to traditional conceptions of social democracy. For over two decades I have been writing about necessary limits to state action and the importance of civil society (see, for instance, my *Models of Democracy*). I see my work as part of a larger effort to rethink social democracy, preserving its focus on liberty and social justice, while remaining flexible about the instruments to achieve these values.

Scruton is concerned that I elide inequality and injustice. Looking back at my essay I can see why he might have this impression. *Global Covenant* – the book which elaborates the arguments of my essay – is clearer on the matter. There the focus is not on equality as such but on social justice focused, in particular, on a concern with the avoidance of serious harm and the remedying of urgent need. In the current context of global politics this principle is already radical enough to generate profound questions about the existing distribution of life chances and about how we need to act, in trade, the environment and many other spheres, to avoid some of the most serious outcomes that profoundly affect the life chances and life expectancy of millions of people.

I find it odd that Scruton thinks I argue against America. America is a wonderful place in many respects! My argument in the openDemocracy debate is about (and against) two dominant United States-led policy packages. These

packages are willed and enforced by the current administration; but they are certainly open to change. My preoccupation is with the way these two policy packages are making
many already acute transnational problems (development,
the environment, security) harder to solve, and thus in part
have become an element of the problems themselves.

Of course US policies are neither the sole origin nor the
main cause of many aspects of the structure and dynamic of contemporary globalization, as I have argued, for
example, with Anthony McGrew and others in *Global
Transformations*. Nor do I argue that 'the market' as such is
to blame for the impoverishment of the world's poorest
countries.

I hold that the current form of market rules and regula-
tions, which strongly favours the developed world, does not
provide adequate access points into the world economy for
the world's poorest countries; and that the building of
political, social and environmental governance capacity –
at local, national and global levels – is a crucial step on the
road to effective development.

East Asia and globalization: Martin Wolf

Martin Wolf's new book, *Why Globalization Works*, makes
many important points in this respect. He and I would
agree that it is not the market alone that generates many of
the worst difficulties faced by the poorest countries, but
that this is the result of a complex mixture of actions,
including the outrageous and hypocritical position that the
US and the European Union take on many trade-related
questions (for example, agriculture and textiles).

But Wolf is hostile to my characterization of the policies
of the Washington Consensus as 'too narrow'. He rejects my
view that the Washington Consensus needs to be thoroughly

overhauled if a focus on sustainable development, the creation of sound political and social institutions and sustained investment in human capital is to be achieved.

Yet this is precisely the direction in which the policy package of the Washington Consensus has itself been reshaped in recent years, although this process has not gone as far as it must. Joseph Stiglitz has made these points well in *Globalization and its Discontents*[3] where he shows how the practice of the Washington Consensus has often led to programmes which have undermined the development of human capital and the protection of the poor during phases of economic adjustment.

Stiglitz also shows that the Washington Consensus's overall policy range is excessively restrictive and that globalization needs to be carefully sequenced and balanced with policies that focus on poverty reduction, social protection and the nurturing of new competitive industries. Quite so. My point about the Washington Consensus is that its policy range is too limited to achieve prosperity, development and renewed human capital investment. What is missing can be addressed.

Wolf's failure to acknowledge the excessive narrowness of the policies of the Washington Consensus goes hand in hand with the claim that the rapid economic successes of Asia can be explained by liberal market thought. What is missing in both cases is an adequate grasp of the complexities of the social and political conditions of development. China has staggered and regulated its entry into the global market. While it has progressively liberalized its trading policy, it has highly regulated capital movements.

In general, China has practised 'governing globalization' and 'sequencing' entry into the global market. This is consistent with the policies of selective openness practised by many East Asian countries, as Stiglitz and many others have pointed out. The development of the East Asian economies is better represented by a theory of staged global market entry, attentive to the complex social and political conditions of any kind of successful entry, rather than by liberal economic philosophy as such.

Development and human security: David Mepham

David Mepham points out that I say little in my essay about multinational companies and how their operations and practices might be better regulated. This is true, but in *Global Covenant* I seek to provide an account of how important it is to reconnect the economic with human rights, and the commercial with the environmental. There is much to be learnt from the global compact in this regard but, as I have just said in response to Cattaui, without some enforcement capacity the compact is vulnerable to failure. I myself argue for a stronger 'reframing' of the market with rules which entrench economic activity in social, welfare and environmental standards.

Mepham also argues that my openDemocracy essay focused too much on the global and too little on domestic issues when it comes to thinking about the problems of development. I agree that the essay has this bias. Mepham argues that alongside a focus on global governance we need a deep analysis of the structures of governance within some developing countries, 'the extent to which these may hinder rather than advance the interests of poor people'. The points he makes on this matter are compelling and I share his view that much can be learnt from initiatives such as the New Partnership for Africa's Development and the UN's Arab Development Report.

A focus on global obstacles to development must not blind us to the importance of developing strong domestic standards with respect to market governance, corporate policies, corruption and the environment. As Mepham also points out, many of the bitter conflicts which constitute obstacles to a state's stability and prosperity have local and regional origins – not necessarily any relation to wider geopolitical structures. Yet overarching global security structures have a profound bearing on how many of these security issues are dealt with. The narrow security doctrine of the current American administration will not provide a security environment that helps tease out and address the political and human rights issues often at stake.

The United Nations and global governance

Wolf, Bhagwati and Scruton do not share my view that the multilateral order is in severe trouble. Clearly, there is room for debate on this question. Kofi Annan's contribution to the discussion is significant. Annan speaks about the way in which the multilateral order faces a set of profound crises around issues of security, solidarity and division. In his judgement, our multilateral system is currently failing three key tests: collective security, solidarity between rich and poor, and mutual respect between faiths and cultures.

Why does it matter if these tests are failed? Kofi Annan is explicit: millions of people will die prematurely and unnecessarily if UN objectives such as the Millennium Development Goals are not met. I share his view. The multilateral order is in trouble. And the trouble is all the more poignant because we do not have to accept its failures; solutions are within our grasp.

The difficulties of the UN system go back to its foundation in 1945. The geopolitical settlement of that year was built into the UN system; the privileges of the great powers were locked into the operational mechanisms of the UN. The UN proclaimed a hugely significant set of cosmopolitan values (concerned with the equal moral worth, equal dignity and rights of every human being) yet spliced these together with the asymmetrical powers of the state system and the realities of sovereignty. The result has been that its cosmopolitan values are only occasionally upheld, the Security Council rules on some emergency situations and not others according to the geopolitical interests at stake, and the legitimacy and effectiveness of the UN are considerably weakened.

The cosmopolitan values entrenched in the UN Charter were painfully articulated in the aftermath of the Holocaust, the horrors of the two world wars, and the separation and the division of Europe. The values remain of enduring significance but the geopolitical settlement of 1945 is the wrong institutional basis to make these values count across the globe.

If the UN were being designed today the Security Council would surely have a very different representative quality; at the very least, Britain and France would not have veto-power status and significant developing countries such as India and Brazil would have more influential positions. Better still, the whole representative basis of the Security Council would be recast to represent all regions on a fair and equal footing. The recent recommendations by Annan's High-level Panel suggest some useful steps in this direction, and they are to be welcomed accordingly.

I agree with aspects of Roger Scruton's reflections that the UN has often legitimated criminal regimes, but I am not sure we agree on the reasons for this. For me, the heart of the problem is the recognition in the UN Charter of sovereignty as effective power, the de facto control over a circumscribed territory. Those who wield such power have often been regarded as the legitimate bearers of public authority irrespective of tests of democracy and human rights.

The position of sovereignty in international law has changed in recent times, as I have documented in some of my recent work (see, for example, the third part of *Global Covenant*). Nonetheless, the recognition of effective power as legitimate power has a highly problematic history, and has led to many brutal regimes being wrongly regarded as equally legitimate members of the international community.

I also agree with Roger Scruton that the reform of the UN must take account of the exceptional position of the US, and must seek to meet some of its legitimate security concerns. Those concerns which focus on the current wave of global terrorism are particularly pressing, and of course are shared by many nations. But it is one thing to take account of the position of the US, and another to write the rules of multilateral coordination and international law according to US interests. The law was never well defined domestically when it was defined to suit the most powerful interests. Why should we accept such a position at the global level?

Many of the problems facing the multilateral order today arise because it does not work fast or effectively enough to resolve many of the pressing issues which affect our lives – from security to poverty and the degradation of the global commons. This matters for precisely the reasons Kofi Annan highlights. The stakes are high, but so too are the potential gains for human security and development if the aspiration to marry liberty and social justice – global social democracy – can be realized.

One thing is clear: existing security and development policies are not working well enough and the case for addressing better many of the critical issues which affect the quality of life of millions of people daily (poverty, HIV/Aids, global warming) is overwhelming. Narcís Serra's contribution to this book, which I will return to below, highlights this well.

Regionalism and globalization: Grahame Thompson

Grahame Thompson makes a number of very telling points of a different kind in his contribution to the exchange. He and I have been debating aspects of global economic change for several years. We disagree on how to characterize and interpret global economic developments on a number of key dimensions, including the role of regionalism. Since I have responded to many of his concerns elsewhere I will not go over this ground now (see, for example, my *Globalization/Anti-Globalization* with Anthony McGrew[4]).

Thompson's emphasis on the importance of regionalism is illuminating, but where we differ is on how far one can characterize economic change as regional or global. In my judgement, regionalization and globalization have been complementary forces over the last few decades. The dominant forms of regionalism remain open to trade from other areas, and have largely been a force easing the access of clusters of countries into the global market. It is not surprising that these processes have been highly uneven, with the result that economic activity is heavily concentrated in some places. To me this illustrates the hierarchical and divisive nature of globalization in its current form – not the establishment of regionalization as such. But more research is needed on these key questions and this will have a bearing on policy as well.

Thompson's remarks on migration and labour markets are well taken. But again there are differences. While migration levels were historically unprecedented between 1880 and 1914, and collapsed in the 1919–39 period, by the early 1990s migration had returned to earlier high levels (see *Global Transformations*). Migration levels are likely to continue to rise as the OECD's population stagnates or declines, and the rest of the world's population rapidly expands. Free labour mobility, as Grahame Thompson points out, is a highly unlikely future, but a new migration regime is an important idea to be explored further.

A more balanced economic agenda would be one that was concerned not just with the movement of goods and services but also labour flows, including of unskilled labour. For example, a relatively small programme of increasing temporary work visas in the developed countries could generate substantial income gains for workers from the poorest countries. Indeed, it has been estimated by Dani Rodrik that such gains would in all probability exceed the predictions for income gains for all of the proposed Doha reforms.

Grahame Thompson and I disagree on the degree of integration of global financial markets. But his emphasis on rising risks in the financial system is important, as is his stress on the troubled relation of the US economy to the rest of the world. The gross imbalances in the international system that arise from the US's unsustainable balance of payments and internal budget deficit are likely to be a serious source of future financial market instability. All the more reason, I think, to consider the deepening of the regulatory structures of the financial system.

In this context, the creation of a world financial authority to monitor and supervise global financial markets and capital flows becomes more urgent, not less. New forms of global governance could be given an impetus from the instabilities and crises of cross-border financial activity.

Towards a new coalition: John Elkington and Takashi Inoguchi

In this regard, John Elkington's essay makes a number of useful remarks. Elkington stresses the urgent need to scale up our practical responses to issues like financial market volatility, HIV/Aids, corruption control, global warming and the likely failure to meet the Millennium Development Goals.

Elkington holds that the current combined efforts of governments, business and civil society seeking to deal with these problems are being outpaced by them, and that we face being overrun. Wisdom dictates a re-examination of the limits of current forms of governance, and the significant democratic and justice deficits they manifest. Is there any political momentum towards a new global covenant that might shift the focus of the global governance agenda from liberty and markets to social justice, solidarity and sustainability?

I think there are strong reasons for believing that a coalition could emerge to push these ideas further. It could comprise a wide range of institutions, groups and forces:

- European countries with strong liberal and social democratic traditions;
- liberal groups in the US which support multilateralism and the rule of law in international affairs;
- developing countries struggling for freer and fairer trade rules in the world economic system;
- non-governmental organizations, from Amnesty International to Oxfam, campaigning for a more just, democratic and equitable world order;
- transnational social movements contesting the nature and form of contemporary globalization;
- those economic forces that desire a more stable and managed global economy.

Will this happen? There are clearly many obstacles to the formation of such a coalition. Yet each of these forces has been concerned in one way or another to develop a more accountable and effective form of global governance. We cannot know now if such a coalition could triumph. But there are many profound reasons why such a coalition should be created, to change the agenda of contemporary globalization.

Takashi Inoguchi's reflections on the way the leading actors in the global system have both different styles and substantive ambitions is a useful reminder, if one were necessary, of the schisms in global politics. In addition, his account of the ad hoc and incremental qualities of agreements such as the Madrid accord, the Kyoto protocol and the Human Rights Declaration rightly draws attention to the different modes of ordering globalization pursued by leading powers. In his account, effective and accountable global governance requires three things – a meeting of minds, a sharing of beliefs and an overlap of interests – all currently missing to varying degrees.

There is, of course, much truth in this, and yet it is not clear what follows. Historical pessimism? The surrender of the policy agenda to dominant geopolitical and geo-economic interests? Neither Inoguchi nor I think this would be the right conclusion. He recognizes that the case for 'a newly synthesized global covenant' is compelling. The global public goods we require for an equitable and just trading system, an accountable and stable financial order, a sustainable environment and so on depend on creating the politics to support a new global covenant. A broad-based coalition is indispensable to building up our efforts in this regard. Moreover, our historical epoch has furnished plenty of examples that extraordinarily progressive efforts are possible, from the peaceful revolution that led to the fall of the Berlin Wall to the end of apartheid in South Africa.

The requirement of legitimacy: Narcís Serra

There is another reason, provided by Narcís Serra, to expect some change in political direction. The Washington

Consensus and security doctrine, as he put it, 'have an Achilles' heel in common which becomes more evident as time goes by. They suffer from a lack of legitimacy.' Legitimacy, although a contested notion, entails recognition by the public that an action or set of actions has been taken by an appropriate authority following accepted legal rules and procedures. As Serra argues, at the international level it has three elementary requirements: compliance with international law and procedures; deliberation and consultation involving the international community; and a commitment to uphold global interests.

Serra's paper is particularly welcome because it shows how legitimacy can only be achieved involving elements of a 'bottom-up approach'. (The position is not the same as Patrick Bond's because it is tied, as I will clarify below, to common rules and procedures.) This is not just a matter of morality but also of effectiveness. As he contends, security cannot be sustained without respect for the human rights of, and involvement of, all those significantly affected by a conflict. Mary Kaldor's contribution in appendix B elaborates this argument in a very important way. In the domain of economics, this position means acknowledging that there is no single set of policies and prescriptions to ensure prosperity, and that in the absence of a single model for development, as Serra says, 'developing countries should have the freedom to experiment with the policies that they consider appropriate to their specific circumstances'. The Barcelona Development Agenda, in appendix A, exemplifies this approach. In line with the arguments that I set out in chapter 1 and here, Serra notes that an appropriate framework of rules, procedures and institutions matters to sustain a legitimate, bottom-up approach to both economic and security policy – and that this, in turn, should be understood as a robust form of multilateralism.

Serra argues that multilateralism must be developed to the point where countries are moved 'to contribute jointly to the production of global public goods'. For Serra, the development of such a multilateralism must begin at home, that is, in Europe. In economic and security policy, he says, 'we must demand a more determined, more responsible attitude on the part of the EU as a "norms promoter"'. Quite so.

Building bridges between cosmopolitanism and nationalism: Anne-Marie Slaughter and Thomas N. Hale

Slaughter and Hale's contribution to the debate decisively moves the argument forward and, in part, on to new terrain. At the heart of their contribution is the contention that if cosmopolitanism and nationalism are treated as mutually exclusive, with the implication being that one must choose one or the other, it will be at the expense of both. Moreover, if the divisions are cast in this way, cosmopolitan forces will lose in the long term to their older and better entrenched rival. Or, to put the point another way, if the worlds of Washington and cosmopolitanism are simply juxtaposed, and US- and Bush-bashing prevails among critics of US policy, then the critics' position will be unnecessarily diminished and both sides will fail to see – even though it is admittedly hard to see – elements of common ground.

At issue is not just rhetoric and style, but key questions of substance. Cosmopolitans must come to understand nationalism as a serious force in the US and, of course, elsewhere. George W. Bush was re-elected in part, Slaughter and Hale argue, because he was seen as 'more patriotic than his opponent' and championed ideals – such as 'Freedom is on the march' – which resonated with his public. And for many Americans this was not 'a cover for the cynical expansion of empire'.

The dichotomy between cosmopolitanism and nationalism must be deconstructed in order to enhance the debate and potential value of both. Clues as to how this can be done can be found in the language of people like Martin Luther King Jr, who combined appeals to Americans with religious and cosmopolitan values. The core of Slaughter and Hale's arguments is a call for a set of 'moral responsibilities' that could appeal to Bush voters and activists concerned with global issues. They put the key point thus: 'Both Christian morality and civic virtue enjoin citizens, especially the powerful, to uphold the rights and freedoms of others. They impose a duty to help the poor, the sick, and the disadvantaged, and they insist on responsible stewardship of God's creation. They require good people to have a decent respect and tolerance for the opinions of others. They teach that pride – jingoism included – is a sin, and that humility is a virtue.'

Slaughter and Hale believe that this shift in attitude and language will help carve out a promising approach to pressing issues such as human trafficking and poverty; and highlight new institutional mechanisms – such as the Canadian Prime Minister's proposal for regular G20 meetings at the leaders' level (L20) – for wider support. At issue is the search for institutional structures which might serve a cosmopolitan agenda while 'recognizing and embracing the power and perspective of different nation-states'.

There is much in this argument to admire. The concept of developing a language of moral responsibilities that might cut across the current dangerous divides is appealing, as is the argument about new state-based mechanisms as vehicles for cosmopolitan ideals. This is a promising set of ideas for coalition building around an urgent global agenda. But we must also recognize limits to its scope and efficacy. First, some issues like HIV/Aids are unlikely to yield a common approach because major differences prevail on contraception and reproductive health care for women. Second, in pressing areas like security we have to contend with fundamental differences of approach – not just between what I call narrow and broad conceptions of security (critical though these are) but also towards international law, agreements and procedures, as Narcís Serra highlights. Thirdly, economic agendas differ, as several of the chapters in this book demonstrate. The differences between the Washington Consensus, the augmented Washington Consensus and a social democratic agenda for globalization are unlikely to be closed by an appeal to common values – systematic differences of interpretation, policy and interest divide them.

Nonetheless, Slaughter and Hale's arguments are worthy of a wide audience, and offer a welcome new mix of considerations in the debate between cosmopolitanism and nationalism, and how to build bridges between them.

Against misrepresentations

I will conclude by responding to points in the openDemocracy debate where I have been misunderstood and misrepresented, for those who have read the whole exchange.

Martin Wolf alleges that I fail to grasp adequately the meaning of the term 'Washington Consensus' and, in particular, the original formulation by John Williamson that did not include the free movement of capital flows. He is wrong. I take considerable trouble to distinguish different senses of the term and I point out explicitly that Williamson excluded free capital mobility.

Wolf seems offended that I make 'a false comparison' between the Washington Consensus and the new Washington security doctrine. But I make no such comparison. My point is that these two very different doctrines, which emerged in distinct time-periods, combine to weaken state capacities, and the abilities of multilateral organizations to solve problems.

Wolf argues that there is no evidence to support the claim that the effects of capital mobility on the poorest countries have been damaging. I cite two studies in the chapter, and further research in *Global Covenant*. He is particularly concerned about my refusal to understand that many problems of development and security today are due to the asymmetrical nature of political power in the interstate system. But I do not see how he can think this. After all, the essay is about the disproportionate power of the 'G1'!

Jagdish Bhagwati (writing in openDemocracy's debate forum)[5] has come to the view that I think trade is harmful to health. I have no idea why he thinks this, or why he thinks the likes of Joseph Stiglitz and Dani Rodrik are 'anti-trade'. He comments negatively on the range of economists I refer to, but if he had only looked at my book he would see that I refer to a diversity of economists, including himself (several times)! His points about my stance towards trade and about the range of economists I refer to do him no credit. He should not name-call and stick to the arguments.

Bhagwati construes my position as hostile to trade, and then says he has strong criticisms to make. I agree that some of the criticisms are strong, but they are not criticisms of me! There are two important issues which he fails to separate: the role of trade liberalization in explaining economic prosperity, growth and inequality; and the general desirability of trade liberalization and related policies.

On the first of these, it seems odd that Bhagwati and Wolf now want to claim the achievements of Chinese economic development for liberal market ideology and open market integration. Margaret Thatcher used to do something similar, claiming that Japan, South Korea and Taiwan were all superb examples of her own political and economic philosophy in practice.

Of course, liberalization has had a significant role, but so have many other factors. Significant tariff liberalization occurred in China, India and elsewhere after substantial domestic economic progress had been made, and after a period of economic take-off. Bhagwati's causal approach here is too simplistic. None of this is to detract, of course, from the view that trade liberalization has been an important impetus to development for low and middle income countries.

Apparently, the liberalization agenda has no responsibility for the economic difficulties of Latin America or Africa because the period in question is not long enough and only one country is a good model: Chile. Interesting! Thus Bhagwati defines as irrelevant to the test of the credibility of the liberalization programme all except one of the countries of these two great continents, and says that the medicine was effective in one 'genuine' case. Chile apparently proves the liberal globalizers right.

However, Chile is not in all respects a good example. True, Chile has cut tariffs substantially, but contrary to the dominant economic medicine it has maintained tight control of capital movements. It is only half a globalizer. Elsewhere in Latin America there are few signs of the liberal globalizing agenda delivering sustainable development (despite many countries following Washington Consensus policies), and there has been continuing economic stagnation or decline across many African countries and several transition economies.

On the second point, Bhagwati holds that my views entail autarky. They do not. As I noted above, trade liberalization has generally been a positive factor in the development of poorer countries. I endorse it, particularly in the context of an impartial rule system that applies to each and every country. The problem is that the current trading system falls radically short of this impartial ideal, as he knows.

I am also strongly in favour of trade liberalization when it is combined with policies aimed at growth, an effective safety net offering social protection during adjustment periods, and well-focused poverty-reduction programmes. These need to be combined with measures offering infant industry protection to developing countries – the kind of protection most, if not all, developed countries have enjoyed in the past. Examples of the successful use of emerging industry protection can be found in South Korea and Taiwan, both of which linked it to performance criteria.

Meghnad Desai's response to my paper seems more than a little peculiar; for in truth it is an account of his own recent book and he only adds a cursory reference to my work at the outset and conclusion of his article.

Desai alleges that the agenda I set out seeks to create a state at the global level and that the project of social democracy is inherently statist. The emphasis of my work is different. I seek to show how political power has been reconfigured in the last few decades and that it is now multilevel and multilayered. My view is that this trend is on balance a positive one because the key political issues we face are themselves increasingly multilevel and multilayered.

However, I seek to defend a democratic and cosmopolitan conception of governance, guided by the principle of inclusiveness and subsidiarity, and concerned to build transparent, open and democratic governance where it is needed. To argue in favour of a strong and impartial trade system, of organizations to deal with global warming, of transnational regulatory structures that can cope with virulent infectious diseases is to argue in favour of a complex of agents and agencies capable of both rule-making and enforcement.

Curiously, Meghnad Desai closes his essay with what seems to me a strong plea for a global state and global democracy. His model of these things seems to me far too federalist, hierarchical and . . . statist! Read some of the cosmopolitan literature, Meghnad!

The way ahead

The core issue, as I see it, is how to transform effectively globalization today. My arguments for cosmopolitan or global social democracy are just one contribution to this discussion, but they seem reasonably robust, at least for now. But the debate will continue: the shortcomings of the Washington security agenda are increasingly apparent, and further work on what comes beyond the Washington (economic) Consensus has never been more important.

Fortunately there is good work – both imaginative and practical – such as the recently developed Barcelona Development Agenda and the proposals by Mary Kaldor and others for a new human security doctrine for Europe – that points a way forward. These new positive formulations are included as appendices to this volume. They help continue and extend the debate.

APPENDIX A

The Barcelona Development Agenda[1]

We, a group of economists from developing and developed countries, have met in Barcelona on September 24 and 25 2004 to consider the prospects for growth and development around the world. We discussed the effects of economic reforms applied by many developing nations over the last two decades, the lessons for economic policy-making that emerge from this experience, and the performance of the international economic system into which poor and middle-income countries are increasingly integrated.

We noted three encouraging trends:

- The gains made by human rights, democracy and the rule of law in many – but regrettably not all – developing nations.
- The growth takeoff in several countries – including India and China – which has the potential to pull tens of millions more people out of poverty.
- The increasing recognition of the importance of macro-economic stability, which for instance has led to a dramatic reduction in inflation in historically inflation-prone Latin America.

But we also noted at least three reasons for concern:

- The recurrence and severity of systemic financial crises affecting developing nations, including some that have undertaken adjustment and stabilization policies following international guidance.
- The mediocre record of reforms in igniting sustained economic growth in many regions of the world.
- The persistence – and often the worsening – of highly unequal distributions of wealth and income in many developing countries.

Our discussion was primarily focused on policy lessons and the need for changes in both rich and poor nations. There was broad agreement on seven sets of lessons, which in turn serve as priorities for reform.

First, both basic economic reasoning and international experience suggest that institutional quality – such as respect for the rule of law and property rights – plus a market orientation with an appropriate balance between market and state, and attention to the distribution of income, are at the root of successful development strategies. Moreover, the institutions that put these abstract principles into reality matter, and developing countries should work hard to improve their institutional environments. But effective institutional innovations are highly dependent on a country's history, culture and other specific circumstances. Encouraging developing nations to copy mechanically the institutions of rich countries – as international financial institutions tend to do – is not guaranteed to yield results, and can do more harm than good.

Second, experience has shown again and again that large debts – both public and private – , poorly regulated banks and loose monetary policies are serious hindrances to development. Not only do these practices fail to stimulate growth in the medium term. They can also expose nations to financial and debt crises that carry tremendous costs, especially for the poor. Developing nations that hope to prosper should therefore pursue prudent financial, monetary, fiscal and debt policies. But a prudent fiscal stance, for instance, is not the same as a balanced budget every year, regardless of circumstances. Macroeconomic policies that are countercyclical are both more efficient and also ultimately more sustainable politically. Developing countries ought to build the institutions to make countercyclical policies feasible. International lending institutions should encourage such policies whenever possible. The macroeconomic accounting frameworks used by these institutions should also have the necessary built-in flexibility – for instance by treating productive infrastructures and R&D investment as asset purchases and not as current expenditures, for a given fiscal target.

Third, there is no single set of policies that can be guaranteed to ignite sustained growth. Nations that have succeeded at this tremendously important task have faced different sets of obstacles and have adopted varying policies regarding regulation, export and industrial promotion, and technological innovation and knowledge acquisition. Countries should be free to experiment with policies suited to their specific circumstances, and international lending organizations and aid agencies should encourage such experimentation. But freedom to experiment is not the same as an 'anything goes' approach to development. Nor should this freedom be used to disguise policies that merely transfer income to politically powerful groups. The priority is to identify the most binding constraints to growth and to address them through microeconomic and macroeconomic policies. Micro interventions should be aimed at redressing specific market failures, and incentives should be contingent on improved performance by recipients.

Fourth, multilateral trade negotiations should proceed in a manner that promotes development. Agricultural and textile protectionism in developed countries represents an important obstacle to the participation of developing countries in the global economy. But some of the developing countries may limit their potential growth through inappropriate trade policies. We encourage a successful conclusion of the Doha Round that will provide more opportunities for world growth, thereby creating more room for developing countries to pursue their own growth strategies.

Fifth, international financial arrangements are not working well. Poor countries remain largely cut off from private financial flows and official aid levels are insufficient. Private capital flows to middle-income countries are highly volatile, and this volatility is largely unrelated to economic fundamentals in the recipient countries. Systemic capital account shocks continue to be common, and contagion increasingly hits countries widely regarded as having sound policies. At the core of the problem is the absence of markets and instruments that would permit a more efficient risk-sharing among countries. Multilateral lending institutions do not do enough to overcome these failings of private financial markets. A focus on 'moral hazard' as the driving force behind crises has diverted attention from other causes of financial instability. Talk of reforming the international financial architecture has produced few tangible results. One reason may be that developing nations' views are under-represented in the decision-making of the multilateral lenders. The allocation of votes in the boards of these institutions still reflects power relations of the past, and has little to do with the present-day weight of countries in the world economy. In short: reforming international financial arrangements should be a priority for rich and poor countries.

Sixth, current international arrangements deal with movements of capital and labor asymmetrically. International financial institutions and G7 governments generally treat capital mobility as something to be encouraged. The same is not true of international labor mobility. But reasons of both equity and efficiency argue for allowing for greater international migration. We need a set of international rules and institutions to guide cross-border movements of people, including guest workers and service providers, and to promote the use of remittances from migrants as an additional source of financing. Improving the rights of migrants will facilitate their integration into the job market and limit exploitation.

Seventh, the worsening of the environment, including problems of global warming, need to be tackled with sustainable development policies at both national and global levels. This is an area in which both rich and poor countries have work to do.

There is much not to like about the state of the world today. The fact that over a billion human beings live in abject poverty should be a cause for unrelenting concern. AIDS and other epidemic diseases represent a tragedy for the least developed countries, mainly in Africa. In the Millennium Development Goals donor nations committed to increase aid to address these and other problems, but that commitment remains largely unfulfilled. It also is easy to be discouraged by the failure of all kinds of magical recipes for development. But concern is not the same as despair. Nor should concern for the poor serve to justify unthoughtful anti-growth attitudes. Over the last half-century a number of countries have pulled themselves out of poverty, and others are doing the same today. There are hopeful lessons to be learned from these experiences, some of which we have tried to summarize in this agenda. Equitable and progressive development paths are conceivable. No set of policies can guarantee success, but we know more today about where to look for the keys to that success.

Citizens of developing countries know full well that development is a long and arduous path. If their leaders embark upon it, and if rich countries help reform international arrangements that hinder rather than ease this path, there is still reason for hope.

Signatories to the Barcelona Development Agenda:

Alice Amsden, Barton L. Weller Professor of Political Economy, Massachusetts Institute of Technology

Olivier Blanchard, Professor of Economics, Massachusetts Institute of Technology

Guillermo Calvo, Chief Economist, Inter-American Development Bank, Washington DC

Ramón Caminal, Professor of Economics, Consejo Superior de Investigaciones Cientificas (CSIC), Madrid

Daniel Cohen, Professor of Economics, Université de Paris (Panthéon-Sorbonne) and École Normale Supérieure, Paris

Antón Costas, Professor of Economics, Consejo Superior de Investigaciones Cientificas (CSIC), Madrid

Guillermo de la Dehesa, Chairman of the Centre for Economic Policy Research (CEPR), London

Jeffrey Frankel, James W. Harpel Professor of Capital Formation and Growth, Kennedy School of Government, Harvard University

Jordi Galí, Director of Centre de Recerca en Economia Internacional (CREI), University Pompeu Fabra, Barcelona

Ricardo Hausmann, Professor of Economic Development, Harvard University

Louka Katseli, Director, Development Center, Organization for Economic Cooperation and Development (OECD), Paris

Martin Khor, Director, Third World Network, Penang

Paul Krugman, Professor of Economics, Princeton University

Deepak Nayyar, Vice-Chancellor, University of Delhi

José Antonio Ocampo, Under-Secretary-General for Economic and Social Affairs, United Nations

Dani Rodrik, Professor of International Political Economy, Kennedy School of Government, Harvard University

Jeffrey D. Sachs, Director, Earth Institute, Columbia University

Miguel Sebastián, Deputy Director, Cabinet Office, Spanish President of Government

Narcís Serra, President of CIDOB Foundation, Barcelona

Joseph E. Stiglitz, Executive Director of Initiative for Policy Dialogue (IPD), Columbia University

Ernesto Talvi, Executive Director, Coalition for Environmentally Responsible Economies (CERES), Boston

Joan Tugores, Principal of the University of Barcelona

Andrés Velasco, Sumitomo-FASID Professor of International Finance and Development, Kennedy School of Government, Harvard University

Jaume Ventura, Professor of Economics, Centre de Recerca en Economia Internacional (CREI), University Pompeu Fabra, Barcelona

Xavier Vives, Professor of Economics and Finance, INSEAD, Paris

John Williamson, Senior Fellow, Institute for International Economics, Washington DC

APPENDIX B

What is Human Security?

Mary Kaldor

Millions of people in the world live in situations of intolerable insecurity, especially in conflict zones like Central and West Africa, the Middle East, the Balkans or Central Asia. In the Democratic Republic of Congo, more than 3 million people have been killed over the last decade, and millions more have been forced to flee their homes. And as has happened in many other places, tens of thousands of women have been raped; gang rapes, rapes of children as young as four and women as old as eighty have been reported, contributing to the HIV/Aids epidemic in the region. Among the Palestinians, people live in daily fear of land seizures, demolition of houses and assassination; the inability to protect one's self, family and property produces an overwhelming sense of humiliation and insecurity. In turn, daily activities like going to the market or to a café have become perilous undertakings for ordinary Israelis because of suicide bombings. In Armenia, Azerbaijan and Georgia, hundreds of thousands of refugees and displaced people are unable to return to their homes or settle, because their lasting insecurity has become a political tool manipulated by politicians in support of their positions in the conflicts. In large parts of Iraq, despite the presence of American forces, dozens of civilian casualties are reported weekly as a result of continuing violent attacks by both insurgents and Coalition forces.

It is these conflicts that become the 'black holes' generating many of the new sources of insecurity that impact
directly on the security of the citizens in other countries. In
the South Caucasus and the Balkans hard drugs and guns
are exported or transported, and there is trafficking or
smuggling of people who are often sexually exploited or
forced to work in the illegal economy. The worsening situation in the Israeli/Palestinian conflict and in Iraq is used
by Islamic militants as evidence of a Judaeo-Christian con-
spiracy against Islam when they are recruiting terrorists.
Wars in Africa defeat Europe's efforts to fight poverty and
disease with development initiatives. Generally, contemporary conflicts are characterized by circumstances of law-
lessness, impoverishment, exclusivist ideologies and the
daily use of violence, which make them fertile ground for a
combination of human rights violations, criminal networks
and terrorism, and this spills over and causes insecurity
beyond the area itself. While these developments may initially have appeared to apply primarily to developing and
conflict states, the 11 September and 11 March attacks in
New York and Madrid have made it clear once and for
all that no citizens of the world are any longer safely
ensconced behind their national borders, and that sources
of insecurity are no longer most likely to come in the form
of border incursions by foreign armies.

Conventional security organizations composed of
armies seem unable to deal with these situations of insecurity. There is a big gap today between existing security organizations and real security needs. This is why individual
countries and multilateral institutions need to adopt
human security policies instead of or as well as state security policies. Human security policies have to be viewed as a
contribution to global security, and, in particular, as a way
of strengthening the United Nations. They require new
principles, new methods and new types of forces that are

different from conventional armies, even though they involve soldiers.

Why human security?

Human security is about the security of individuals and communities rather than the security of states and it combines both human rights and human development, freedom from fear and freedom from want. In the Report of the Commission on Human Security, Amartya Sen conceptualizes human security as narrower than either human development or human rights. In relation to human development, he focuses on the 'downside risks': 'the insecurities that threaten human survival or the safety of daily life, or imperil the natural dignity of men and women, or expose human beings to the uncertainty of disease and pestilence, or subject vulnerable people to abrupt penury'. In relation to human rights, he sees them as 'a class of human rights' that guarantee 'freedom from basic insecurities – new and old'.[1] Thus human security could be conceptualized as incorporating minimum core aspects of both human development and human rights.

The case for adopting a human security approach is threefold. The first reason has to do with morality. It derives from our common humanity. In a world of global communications, we cannot claim we do not know when human beings suffer in other parts of the world. The point made by Kant in 1795, that the global community had shrunk to the point where 'a right violated anywhere is felt everywhere' is even more true today. A second reason is legal. In the aftermath of the Second World War, states signed up to a series of conventions, treaties and declarations that amount to a legal commitment to human security worldwide. Articles 55 and 56 of the United Nations Charter enjoin states to promote *universal* respect for, and observance of, human rights. This obligation is restated in various human rights treaties. In its proposed new constitution, the European Union explicitly recognizes the same obligation. Article 4 states:

In its relations with the wider world, the Union shall uphold and promote its values and interests. It shall contribute to peace, security, the sustainable development of the earth, solidarity and mutual respect among peoples, free and fair trade, eradication of poverty and protection of human rights and in particular children's rights, as well as to strict observance and development of international law, including respect for the principles of the United Nations Charter.

Contemporary states, especially in Europe, therefore, do recognize that they have obligations concerning the human security of people outside its borders.

Finally, and perhaps most convincingly, there is a powerful 'enlightened self-interest' case for the adoption of a human security policy. In the context of 'new wars', the security of individuals in advanced industrial countries as well as elsewhere depends on global security. National borders are no longer the dividing line between security and insecurity: insecurity gets exported. As President Chirac put it in describing the new French military doctrine, the 'first lines of defence' are now far beyond national borders.[2]

In a globalized world the brutalization of a society, with daily experience of high levels of violence and the cheapening of human life, is bound to affect other societies. Dealing with terrorism and organized crime only by devising more robust punitive and intelligence measures within our borders, which may in fact endanger democratic values and institutions, can never be more than fire-fighting. The only real response to such threats is to address the security needs of people in situations of severe insecurity.

The principles of human security

Terms do matter. While there is already a recognition by many politicians that poverty is relevant to security, a holistic approach is still lacking, and there tends to be competition between 'hard' and 'soft' approaches. Human security is about protecting the safety and livelihoods of individuals. Hence it is more robust and comprehensive than the term 'peace', and yet different from the more military approach taken by the United States and by traditional nation-states. It is a 'hard' security policy but it operates on new principles more akin to law enforcement. It means using force in cases of threatened humanitarian catastrophes such as genocide or massive ethnic cleansing – but the ways in which force is used, the means, are as important as the goals. Adoption of the language would both help to mobilize public support and at the same time offer the basis for a set of principles that could guide and streamline policy.

In elaborating the notion of human security, it is possible to identify a set of principles which elucidate the ways in which such an approach differs from conventional approaches to security and development. These principles apply both to 'freedom from fear', i.e. the goal of public safety, and 'freedom from want', i.e. the goal of human development.

The principles do not only apply to hot conflict situations. A distinction is often drawn between the 'prevention' of crises and post-conflict reconstruction. But it is often difficult to distinguish between different phases of conflict precisely because there are no clear beginnings or endings and because the conditions that cause conflict – fear and hatred, a criminalized economy that profits from violent methods of controlling assets, weak illegitimate states, or the existence of warlords and paramilitary groups – are often exacerbated during and after periods of violence. The situation in Palestine, for instance, was supposed to be 'post-conflict' after the Oslo accords, but it has clearly reverted to being in the midst of conflict. The conflicts of the South Caucasus used to be called 'frozen', but 'festering' might have been a better characterization. The principles for a human security policy should therefore apply to a continuum of phases of varying degrees of violence that always involves elements of both prevention and reconstruction.

Principle 1: The primacy of human rights

The primacy of human rights is what distinguishes the human security approach from traditional state-based approaches. Although the principle seems obvious, there are deeply held and entrenched institutional and cultural obstacles that have to be overcome if it is to be realized in practice. Human rights include economic and social rights as well as political and civil rights. This means that human rights such as the right to life, the right to housing, or the right to freedom of opinion are to be respected and protected even in the midst of conflict.

This has profound implications both for security policy and for development. In security terms, the central preoccupation of both practitioners and analysts of foreign policy in recent years has been with the conditions under which human rights concerns should take precedence over sovereignty. This debate often neglects the issue of the means to be adopted in so-called human rights operations. This is especially important where military means are likely to be deployed. It is often assumed that the use of military force is justifiable if there is legal authority to intervene (*ius ad bellum*), and the goals are worthwhile. However, the methods adopted must also be appropriate and, indeed, may affect the ability to achieve the goal specified. In other words, the *how* is as important as the *why*. Unless it is absolutely necessary *and* it has a legal basis, personnel deployed on human security missions must avoid killing, injury and material destruction.

In a war, soldiers may try to minimize civilian casualties but this is secondary to the goal of defeating the enemy. Hence in wars, there is a hierarchy of lives – soldiers try to minimize civilian casualties on their own side, then themselves, then civilians on the other side, and then finally enemy soldiers. In a human security operation, all lives have equal value and human security forces, like police or fire-fighters, may risk their lives to save others, whatever their nationality.

The primacy of human rights also implies that those who commit gross human rights violations are treated as individual criminals rather than collective enemies. In development terms, the primacy of human rights means the primacy of human development as opposed to the growth of national economies. This has profound implications for development policies as well as for more specific issues such as conditionality. Ways have to be found to help the individual even where a country has poor governance or fails to meet various forms of conditionality. Sanctions may therefore be problematic. Different voices within a country should be consulted on the use of conditionality, and means have to be found to assist communities that bypass local authorities.

Principle 2: Legitimate political authority

The end goal of a human security strategy has to be the establishment of legitimate political authority capable of upholding human security. Again this applies both to physical security, where the rule of law and a well-functioning system of justice are essential, and to material security, where increasing legitimate employment or providing infrastructure and public services requires state policies. Legitimate political authority does not necessarily need to mean a state; it could consist of local government or regional or international political arrangements. Since state failure is often the primary cause of conflict, the reasons for state failure have to be taken into account in reconstructing legitimate political authority.[3]

Diplomacy, sanctions, the provision of aid, and civil society links are all among the array of instruments available to states and international institutions aimed at influencing political processes in other countries – opening up authoritarian regimes, strengthening legitimate forms of political authority, and promoting inclusive political solutions to conflict – as is the capacity to deploy civilian personnel. It is in cases of impending humanitarian catastrophe, a threatened genocide for example, that military forces may need to be used. In such cases, they can only succeed on the basis of local consent and support (this is, of course, not the same as consent of the local political authorities who may be responsible for the catastrophe). The most that can be achieved through the use of military forces is to stabilize the situation so that a space can be created for a political or judicial process. Again, this is a difficult cognitive shift for the military since they tend to see their roles in terms of defeating an enemy.

Principle 3: Multilateralism

A human security approach has to be global. Hence it can only be implemented through multilateral action. Multilateralism means more than simply 'acting with a group of states'. In that narrow sense, nearly all international initiatives might be considered multilateral. Multilateralism is closely related to legitimacy and is what distinguishes a human security approach from neocolonialism.

First, multilateralism means a commitment to work with international institutions, and through the procedures of international institutions. This means, first and foremost, working within the United Nations framework, but it also entails working with or sharing out tasks among other regional organizations such as the Organization for Security and Cooperation in Europe and the North Atlantic Treaty Organization in Europe, the African Union, the Southern African Development Community and the Economic Community of West African States in Africa, or the Organization of American States in the Western hemisphere.

Secondly, multilateralism entails a commitment to creating common rules and norms, solving problems through rules and cooperation, and enforcing the rules. It means the extension of international law. Nowadays, legitimate political authority has to be situated within a multilateral framework. Indeed state failure is partly to be explained in terms of the failure of traditionally unilateralist states to adapt to multilateral ways of working.

Thirdly, multilateralism has to include coordination, rather than duplication or rivalry. An effective human security approach requires coordination between intelligence, foreign policy, trade policy, development policy and security policy initiatives of the states and of other multilateral actors, including the United Nations, the World Bank, the IMF and regional institutions. Preventive and pro-active policies cannot be effective if they are isolated and even contradictory.

Principle 4: The bottom-up approach

Notions of 'partnership', 'local ownership' and 'participation' are already key concepts in development policy. These concepts should also apply to security policies. Decisions about the kind of security and development policies to be adopted, whether or not to intervene with military forces or through various forms of conditionality, and how, must take account of the most basic needs identified by the people who are affected by violence and insecurity. This is not just a moral issue; it is also a matter of effectiveness. People who live in zones of insecurity are the best source of intelligence. Thus communication, consultation and dialogue are essential tools for both development and security.

Particularly important in this respect is the role of women's groups. The importance of gender equality for development, especially the education of girls, has long been recognized. The same may be true when managing conflict. Women play a critical role in contemporary conflicts, both in dealing with the everyday consequences of the conflict and in overcoming divisions in society. Involvement and partnership with women's groups could be a key component of a human security approach.

Principle 5: Regional focus

New wars have no clear boundaries. They tend to spread through refugees and displaced persons, through minorities who live in different states, through criminal and extremist networks. Indeed most situations of severe insecurity are located in regional clusters. The tendency to focus attention on areas that are defined in terms of statehood has often meant that relatively simple ways of preventing the spread of violence are neglected. Time and again, foreign policy analysts have been taken by surprise when, after considerable attention had been given to one conflict, another conflict would seemingly spring up out of the blue in a neighbouring state.

By the same token, a regional focus is important in restoring and/or fostering economic and trade cooperation.

The breakdown of transport and trade links associated with war is often a primary reason for falls in production and employment that contribute to poverty and insecurity.

Policy proposals

Ideally, a human security approach should be adopted by multilateral institutions. It is uncontroversial to note that current geopolitical circumstances do not make this likely. For historic and symbolic reasons, moreover, there may be a case for individual states or even for more traditional collective security arrangements to sustain their commitment to the defence of borders, although many of the proposals outlined below are applicable in a national context as well. Much more probable is that a human security approach could be adopted by the European Union. The European Union represents a new type of polity; it is neither an intergovernmental institution nor a new nation-state in the making. Its security and development policies will determine its identity in the future. The adoption of a human security approach would demonstrate the EU commitment to global security.

An expanded international political and legal presence

It is very important to have a substantial international presence on the ground in areas of actual or potential insecurity. This is needed for early warning and to acquire local knowledge to help guide policy. The problems of long-distance intelligence have been graphically illustrated in Iraq and Afghanistan. Human intelligence based on engagement with local people can be supplemented by more traditional intelligence methods (technology and espionage) but should increasingly be considered the centrepiece of intelligence.

It is possible to envisage new tools like, for example, the EU monitoring missions. The EU monitoring mission in the former Yugoslavia was important both as a source of intelligence and as a way of providing reassurance on the ground and, possibly, preventing some abuse. Monitoring missions could be deployed in areas of severe insecurity, for example the Middle East or the South Caucasus.

Another proposal is to establish law shops or citizens' advice bureaux in areas of actual or potential insecurity to enable the local population to get legal advice about their rights and how to defend them.

In so far as monitoring missions or advice bureaux are staffed by international personnel, it is also important to create institutions to make their behaviour accountable to a local population. International missions should be accompanied by an independent Ombudsperson facility where the local population could seek information or complain about the policies and practices of international personnel.

A human security response force

In order to increase the effectiveness of international institutions, it would be important to establish combined military and civilian forces whose job is to protect civilians in situations of severe insecurity and which could make a significant contribution to the effectiveness of the United Nations.

In the report of the Study Group on European Security Capabilities,[4] it is proposed that the EU should establish a Human Security Response Force composed of 15,000 personnel, of which one-third would be civilian, as a standing contribution to UN operations. The force would be under the overall direction of the new foreign minister envisaged in the new constitution. It would be composed of a civil-military core with capabilities for planning, intelligence and facilitating deployment; there would be 5,000 personnel at a high state of readiness constantly training and exercising together and a further 10,000 at a lower state of readiness. The force would be based on building blocks already in place. Thus the military component of the force would consist of dedicated national troops, already promised under the Headline Goals agreed at the Helsinki summit in 2001, and civilians (police, legal experts, development experts) also committed under the civilian Headline Goals. The force would be able to deploy smaller human security task forces of around 1,500 people at very short notice. These would be akin to the battle groups but the balance of military and civilians would vary according to the situation.

The force would be largely composed of professionals but it could be supplemented by a Human Security Volunteer Force, who could be either mid-career professionals interested in making a contribution to humanity, or school-leavers. They would volunteer for two years. As well as improving the capacity to mobilize civilian capabilities, the volunteer force would provide a way of increasing popular engagement with EU security policy.

A Human Security Response Force would operate in quite different ways from either traditional peacekeeping or traditional armies. Its main job would be to act in support of law enforcement so it would be more like a police force, although more robust. The principles described above, such as primacy of human rights, the establishment of legitimate political authority or the bottom-up approach, would all shape the way the force was used. The aim should be to protect people and minimize all casualties. This is more akin to the traditional approach of the police, who risk their lives to save others, even though they are prepared to kill *in extremis*, as human security forces should be.

In financial terms, the defence element of a proposed human security force could be covered through restructuring existing European defence budgets. Currently, Europe has 1.8 million men under arms and spends approximately 180 billion euros on defence, so this should not be too difficult to accomplish. Spending on the civilian component should be increased and paid for out of the Common Foreign and Security Policy (CFSP) budget, and development assistance would also need to be increased. In the longer run, a big difference would be made if member states could allocate a part of the defence budgets to the CFSP so that decisions about when and how to use the human security force were at the discretion of those responsible for the CFSP.

A force of 15,000 is quite small in relation to global insecurity. The idea is to start small so that the force can be expanded in the future. The primary purpose of the force is to be able to act in situations of severe human insecurity (genocide, starvation, massive violations of human rights) under UN authorization, so as to strengthen international law and multilateralism. Such a force would also symbolize the distinctive character of the European Union as a new type of multilateral polity.

A similar approach should be adopted by other multilateral institutions, especially the United Nations.

A legal framework

The capacity of international institutions, especially the EU, to act as 'norms-promoters', operating within international law, furthering international law and using legal instruments to enhance security, is hindered by the absence of a single and coherent body of international law governing foreign deployments. It is important to tackle these deficits in the international legal system and encourage the development of a multilateral legal framework covering international human security missions. Such a framework would include both the legality of deployments per se, and the legal regimes that govern deployed personnel, military and civilian, and locals in a conflict area. This would need to build on the domestic law of the host state, the domestic law of the sending states and the rules of engagement, international criminal law, human rights law and international humanitarian law.

Conclusion

The sixtieth anniversary of the liberation of Auschwitz raised questions about the responsibility of the Allies as well as Germany. Their priority was to defeat Germany. Should they not have done more to try to save Jews and gypsies, by bombing the concentration camps, for example, or the railway lines that led to them? In the past, conventional thinking about security focused on strategic assets like oil, and strategic threats posed by enemy states. The security of the lives of human beings outside our own borders was conceived as an ethical issue, in the realm of human rights or development cooperation, but without relevance to the security of those inside borders. In a global context, the difference between the inside and the outside is withering away.

Human security is not simply about 'soft' idealistic concerns. It is about our real physical security wherever we live. If we do not extend the inside world of law and politics outwards, the outside world of anarchy and war will affect us all.

Here, I have focused on policies aimed at physical security, 'freedom from fear'. But it goes without saying that these cannot be disentangled from policies aimed at human development, 'freedom from want'. In particular, the close interrelation between physical and material insecurity in war zones suggests new approaches towards development in general. Key priorities in conflict zones are jobs, the creation of sustainable institutions, public works and public services, security sector reform and disarmament and demobilization. Without such policies in place, young men often have no choice but to join a criminal gang or a paramilitary organization. Reconstruction in war-torn places may provide a new model for development policies which could supplant the current emphasis on such issues as macroeconomic stabilization, privatization or liberalization, which have often, unwittingly, contributed to state failure.

Notes

1 Globalization: The Dangers and the Answers

1 This chapter explores themes examined at greater length in my *Global Covenant: The Social Democratic Alternative to the Washington Consensus* (Cambridge: Polity, 2004). I would like to thank Robert Wade, Jonathan Perraton and Mathias Koenig-Archibugi for criticism of earlier drafts; also Dani Rodrik for permission to use his account of the elements of the augmented Washington Consensus in the box on p. 35.

2 John Williamson, *Latin American Adjustment: How Much has Happened?* (Washington DC: Institute for International Economics, 1990).

3 John Williamson, 'The Washington Consensus and beyond', *Economic and Political Weekly*, 38: 15 (2003).

4 Branko Milanovic, 'Two faces of globalization: against globalization as we know it', *World Development*, 31: 4 (2003), p. 679.

5 Geoffrey Garrett, 'Globalization and inequality', *Perspectives on Politics* (forthcoming).

6 Joseph Stiglitz, 'Distant voices', *Guardian*, 11 Mar. 2004.

7 E. S. Prasad et al., 'Effects of financial globalization on developing countries' (2003), at www.imf.org/external/pubs/nft/op/220/index.htm.

8 Robert Wade, 'The disturbing rise in poverty and inequality', in D. Held and M. Koenig-Archibugi (eds), *Taming Globalization* (Cambridge: Polity, 2003).

9 Ibid.

10 Dani Rodrik, 'The global governance of trade as if development really mattered' (2001), at www.undp.org/bdp, see p. 22.
11 Ibid., p. 12.
12 Mary Kaldor, *New and Old Wars* (Cambridge: Polity, 1998).
13 John Ruggie, 'Taking embedded liberalism global', in Held and Koenig-Avchibugi, *Taming Globalization*, pp. 93–4.

2 The Case for Optimism

1 Martin Wolf, *Why Globalization Works* (New Haven and London: Yale University Press, 2004).

4 The Limits to Globalization

1 'The man who built the WTO: an interview with Peter Sutherland' (12 Jan. 2004), at www.opendemocracy.net/debates/article.jsp?id=3&debateId=52&articleId=1674.

6 Social Democracy as World Panacea?

1 Meghnad Desai, *Marx's Revenge* (London: Verso, 2004).
2 Donald Sassoon, *One Hundred Years of Socialism: The West European Left in the Twentieth Century* (London: I. B. Tauris, 1996).

7 The Test of Practice

1 'The man who built the WTO'.
2 'Making "global" and "ethical" rhyme: an interview with Mary Robinson' (9 Dec. 2003), at www.opendemocracy.net/debates/article.jsp?id=3&debateId=122&articleId=1627.

8 Top Down or Bottom Up?

1 David Held, *Democracy and the Global Order* (Cambridge: Polity, 1995).

2 R. Brenner, *The Boom and the Bubble* (London: Verso, 2003); R. Pollin, *Contours of Descent: US Economic Fractures and the Landscape of Global Austerity* (London: Verso, 2003); J. Foster, *Ecology against Capitalism* (New York: Monthly Review Press, 2002); E. Wood, *Empire of Capital* (London: Verso, 2003); R. Biel, *The New Imperialism* (London: Zed Books, 2000); H. Shutt, *The Trouble with Capitalism* (London: Zed Books, 1999). Earlier studies describing the onset of crisis include S. Clarke, *Keynesianism, Monetarism and the Crisis of the State* (Aldershot: Edward Elgar, 1988), pp. 279–360; D. Harvey, *The Condition of Postmodernity* (Oxford: Blackwell, 1989), pp. 180–97; and E. Mandel, 'Theories of crisis: an explanation of the 1974–82 cycle', in M. Gottdiener and N. Komninos (eds), *Capitalist Development and Crisis Theory: Accumulation, Regulation and Spatial Restructuring* (London: Macmillan, 1989), pp. 30–58.

3 D. Harvey, *The New Imperialism* (Oxford and New York: Oxford University Press, 2003). See also D. Harvey, *Limits to Capital* (London: Verso, 1999); M. Perelman, *The Invention of Capitalism: Classical Political Economy and the Secret History of Primitive Accumulation* (Durham, N.C.: Duke University Press, 2000).

4 I. Bakker and S. Gill, 'Ontology, method and hypotheses', in I. Bakker and S. Gill (eds), *Power, Production and Social Reproduction* (Basingstoke: Palgrave Macmillan, 2003), p. 36.

5 L. Panitch and S. Gindin, 'Global capitalism and American empire', in L. Panitch and C. Leys, *Socialist Register 2004* (London: Merlin Press; New York: Monthly Review Press, 2003).

6 A robust political economic argument along the lines above would not accept the reading of the post-1945 reorganization of global capitalism that Held celebrates as 'a concerted international effort to affirm the importance of universal principles, human rights and the rule of law in the face of strong temptations simply to ratify an overt system of great power interests favouring only some countries and nations'. No doubt there were well-meaning internationalists hard at work, but John Maynard Keynes was so resoundingly defeated – while

attempting to construct a fair Bretton Woods system, in the face of US intransigence - as to cause two heart attacks and his premature death (after a follow-up 1946 meeting in Savannah). Surely, too, the Soviet threat was partly the basis for United Nations expansive human rights rhetorics (and indeed that's all those fine words drafted in the 1948 covenant have ever really amounted to). The capitalist world's ruling classes – many of which had collaborated with Nazism – were in such a weak state by that point that making some liberal-enlightenment concessions was necessary to regain legitimacy.

7 H.-J. Chang and I. Grabel, *Reclaiming Development: An Alternative Economic Policy Manual* (London: Zed Books, 2004).

8 See e.g. Carbon Trade Watch, *The Sky is Not the Limit: The Emerging Market in Greenhouse Gases* (Amsterdam: Transnational Institute, 2003), at www.tni.org.

9 W. Bello, *Deglobalization: Ideas for a New World Economy* (London: Zed Books, 2002).

10 G. Esping-Andersen, *The Three Worlds of Welfare Capitalism* (Princeton: Princeton University Press, 1991).

11 Three Modes of Ordering amidst Globalization

1 Anne-Marie Slaughter, *A New World Order* (Princeton: Princeton University Press, 2004).

2 Robert Jackson, *The Global Covenant: Human Conduct in a World of States* (Oxford and New York: Oxford University Press, 2003).

3 Michael Mann, *Incoherent Empire* (London and New York: Verso, 2003).

4 John R. Talbott, *Where America Went Wrong: And How to Regain her Democratic Ideals* (London: Financial Times/ Prentice Hall, 2004).

14 Three Crises and the Need for American Leadership

1 This text is an edited version of the UN Secretary-General Kofi Annan's commencement address at Harvard University on 10 June 2004.
2 The panel has now reported; see 'A more secure world: our shared responsibility', Report of the Secretary-General's High-Level Panel on Threats, Challenges and Change (Dec. 2004), at www.un.org/secureworld/.

15 What are the Dangers and the Answers?

1 Jagdish Bhagwati's essay could not be included in this volume, but can be found at www.opendemocracy.net/ forums/ thread.jspa?forumID=129&threadID=43264&tstart=0.
Since he raises important questions about trade and trade policy, I will respond to his concerns here along with those of my other critics.
2 David Held, Anthony McGrew, David Goldblatt and Jonathan Perraton, *Global Transformations: Politics, Economics and Culture* (Cambridge: Polity, 1999).
3 Joseph Stiglitz, *Globalization and its Discontents* (New York: W. W. Norton, 2002).
4 David Held and Anthony McGrew, *Globalization/Anti-Globalization* (Cambridge: Polity, 2002).
5 See note 1 above.

Appendix A: The Barcelona Development Agenda

1 This appendix is the final communiqué from a meeting of economists at the Barcelona Forum, 2004. The statement is supported by all the economists whose names are listed at its end.

Appendix B: What is Human Security?

1 Amartya Sen in Commission on Human Security, *Human Security Now* (New York: United Nations, 2003), pp. 8–9.

2 Quoted in B. Boëne and M. L. Martin, 'France: in the throes of epoch-making change', in C. C. Moskos, J. A. Williams and D. R. Segal (eds), *The Post-modern Military: Armed Forces after the Cold War* (London and New York: Oxford University Press, 2000).

3 See Herbert Wulf, 'The challenges of re-establishing a public monopoly of violence', in M. Glasius and M. Kaldor (eds), *A Human Security Doctrine for Europe: Project, Principles, Practicalities* (Oxford: Routledge, forthcoming 2005).

4 This is a summary of the proposals contained in *A Human Security Doctrine for Europe*, The Barcelona Report of the Study Group on European Security Capabilities (2004), available at www.lse.ac.uk/Depts/global/Human%20Security%20Report%20Full.pdf.

Index